Learn to Remember

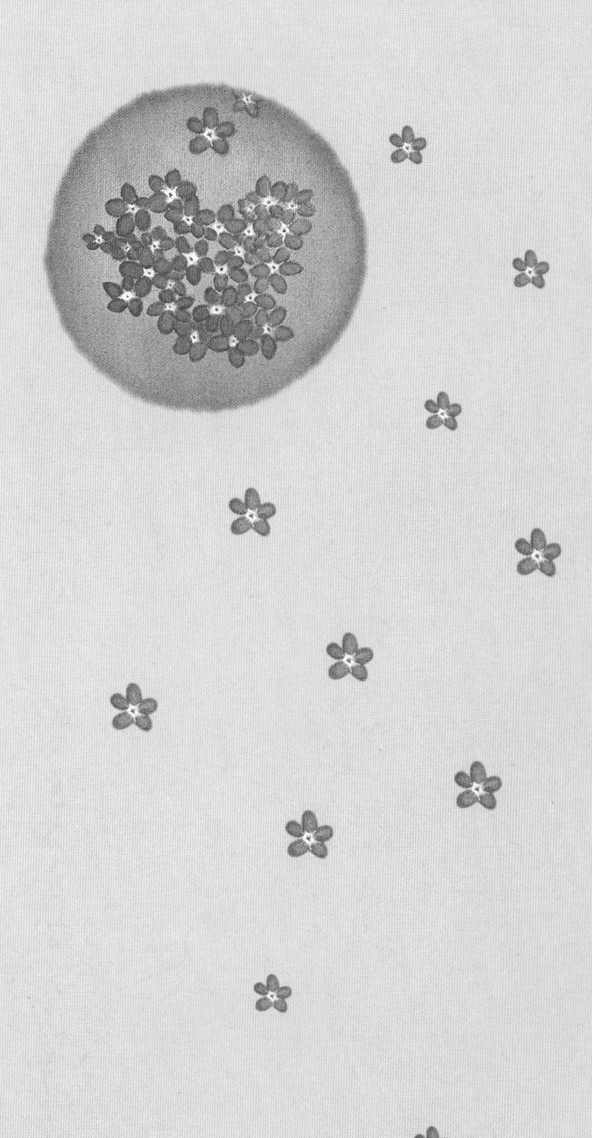

Learn to Remember

Practical Techniques and Exercises to Improve Your Memory

Dominic O'Brien

CHRONICLE BOOKS
SAN FRANCISCO

Learn to Remember

Dominic O'Brien

First published in the United States in 2000 by Chronicle Books LLC

Conceived, created, and designed by
Duncan Baird Publishers Ltd.
Sixth Floor, Castle House
75–76 Wells Street
London W1P 3RE

Typeset in Nofret
Printed in Singapore

Library of Congress Cataloging-in-Publication Data available.

ISBN: 0-8118-2715-1

Associate Author: Donna Dailey
Commissioned color artwork: Mandy Pritty
Commissioned line artwork: Jeniffer Harte
Cover design: Laura Lovett
Cover illustration: Mandy Pritty

Distributed in Canada by
Raincoast Books
9050 Shaughnessy Street
Vancouver, BC V6P 6E5

3 5 7 9 10 8 6 4 2

Chronicle Books LLC
85 Second Street
San Francisco, CA 94105

www.chroniclebooks.com

Dedication

This book is dedicated to
everyone who takes part in mind sports.

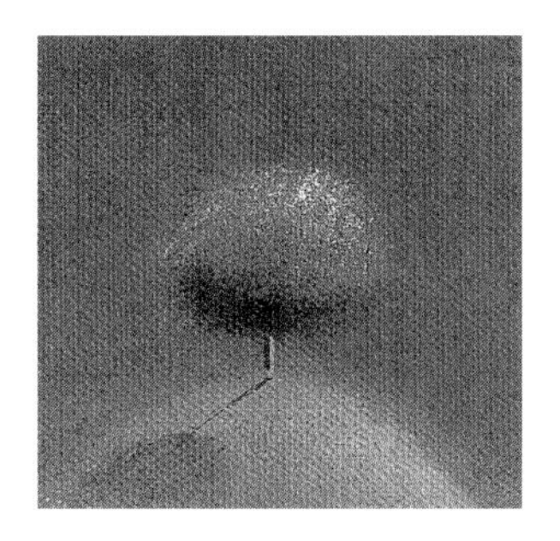

Contents

Introduction 8

A Brief History of Memory 12

From ancient times to the modern age

Oral Traditions 14

The Ancient Greeks 16

The Ancient Romans 18

Memory's Changing Fortunes 19

Memory in Modern Times 22

The Memory Maze 24

How memory works

The Landscape of the Mind 26

Exercise one: Catching the "Jizz" 29

Left Brain, Right Brain 30

Waves of Memory 32

Types of Memory 34

How Memories are Created 40

Exercise two: Finding Your Digit Span 43

The Reliability of Memory 44

Exercise three: Hosting a Memory Forum 47

Sleep, Dreams and Memory 48

Memory and Learning 50

Theories of Forgetting 52

Lost Memory 54

Memory in Children 56

Memory and Aging 58

Enticing the Echoes 60

How to improve your memory

The Memory Gymnasium 62

The Art of Memory 64

The Art of Imagination 68

Exercise four: Painting a Memory Masterpiece 71

The Art of Association 72

The Art of Location 74

The Art of Concentration 76

Exercise five: A Memory Meditation Warm-up 77

The Art of Observation 78

Exercise six: Noticing the Details 79

Revision and Repetition 80

Memory and Health 82

Memory and the Senses 84

Exercise seven: The Memory Kaleidoscope 85

Memory and Music 86

Exercise eight: Staging a Memory Concert 87

The Art of Recall 88

Memory with a Map 92

Discovering memory techniques

Mnemonics 94

Visual Pegs 96

Exercise nine: The Memory Forest 10-note Keyboard 97

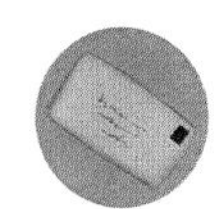
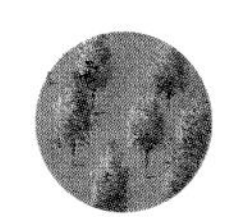

The Story Method 98
Exercise ten: Making a Memory Chain 99
Exercise eleven: Weaving a Narrative Spell 101
The Journey Method 102
Exercise twelve: Walking the Walk 105
Exercise thirteen: The Memory House 107
The Dominic System 108
The Number-Shape System 110
Mind Maps 112

Memory in Action 114
Memory techniques for everyday life

Matching Names and Faces 116
Exercise fourteen: What's in a Name? 117
Keeping a Date 118
Exercise fifteen: Using a Mental Diary 119
Finding the Right Word 120
Exercise sixteen: Crossword Heaven 121
Making Speeches 122
Memory and Games 124
Exercise seventeen: Memorizing Cards of Chance 127
Memory at School 128
Reading and Retaining 130
Exercise eighteen: Evaluate, Assimilate, Remember 131
Speed Reading 132
Exercise nineteen: Checking the Sense 133
Quick-fix Retrieval 134
Exercise twenty: Clearing the Sea-bed of Memory 135

The Memory Palace 136
Gain fulfilment through memory

Living Through Detail 138
Memory Massage 140
Dealing with Life's Demands 142
Exercise twenty-one: The Interview Journey 143
Time Travelling 144
Exercise twenty-two: Harnessing Schooldays 145
Releasing the Past 146
Exercise twenty-three: Disarming a Memory 147
The World of Emotions 148
Exercise twenty-four: Rekindling the Flame 149
Keeping the Mind Young 150
Exercise twenty-five: Tracing Connections 151
Memory of the Future 152

Bibliography 154
Index 156
Acknowledgments 160

 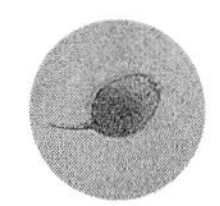    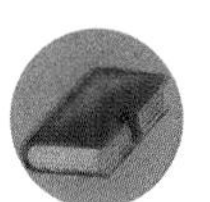

INTRODUCTION

"Hi, Dominic. How come you're entering this year? I hear you're forty-two years old." This was the question asked of me by a seventeen-year-old American student on the first day of the 1999 World Memory Championships. I was told that he had been training his memory for six hours a day for the past six months and was in London for one reason and one reason only: to become World Memory Champion.

Although I believe his opening question was part gamesmanship, many people would argue that this was, in fact, a fair comment. A bright, seventeen-year-old college student should certainly have the edge over a forty-two-year-old codger like me. After all, isn't the memory capacity of a human being supposed to decline with age?

Up until 1988, if someone had asked me that question, I would certainly have answered "yes". In giving that answer, I would have been echoing a popular misconception about memory – that old age and forgetfulness are synonymous. But, in 1988, I was to witness an event that would change my life. I watched a man called Creighton Carvello memorize a randomly shuffled deck of playing cards in just under three minutes – a feat of memory which put his name in

the record books. I was dumbstruck. How could anyone connect 52 unconnected pieces of data together, perfectly in sequence, using nothing but their brain, in such a short space of time? Inspired and fuelled by a burning desire to uncover Creighton's secret, I armed myself with a deck of cards and began a three-month investigation into the potential of my own memory. What followed was an object lesson in accelerated learning. A process of natural selection took place as I threw out ideas that failed and refined techniques that produced results. As each day passed I felt as though I was awakening a giant within me. For the first time in my life, not just my memory, but also my powers of concentration and imagination, were beginning to reveal a potential that I never before realized they had. Unwittingly, I was discovering the art of memory and memory techniques as practised by the ancient Greeks more than two thousand years ago.

After three months of memory training I felt that I had been given a new brain. Soon after, I was entering the record books myself by memorizing not one, but *six* randomly shuffled decks of playing cards from a single sighting of each card. While I was amazed and impressed by my own brain's capacity, I felt at the same time immensely bitter that I had never been taught these same levels of mental agility when I was student struggling with examinations.

As a child, I was diagnosed as dyslexic. In addition, I was described as having an inability to concentrate on and remember what my teachers were saying. As a result, I did not shine academically, and I left school at sixteen. What a shame that I was never shown the techniques described in this book. Even today, when we know comparatively so much more about the brain and the processes of learning, children are not taught how to learn effectively. Why? I have to confess that the answer to that question escapes me.

For the past few decades we have been concentrating on toning our bodies to make them appear beautiful; and we have been tuning our diets and lifestyles to keep ourselves physically healthy. With the advent of a new millennium, it now seems appropriate that we start nurturing, exercising and keeping healthy the command and control centre of our physical selves – the brain.

My hope is that by reading the text and experimenting with the exercises in this book you too will discover the giant within you – and what a giant!

And, by the way, that forty-two-year-old went on to collect a sixth World Memory Championship title.

Dominic O'Brien, December 1999

Setting Your Sights

On the first day of your memory training, you may remember only two or three items from a list. By the next day, you may recall as many as 10; by the following week, 20. Here are a few world records to aspire to!

At the 1999 World Memory Championships I memorized the order of 18 decks of shuffled cards (936) in one hour without a single error, setting a new world record. I also hold the current record for perfectly memorizing a 74-digit number, spoken to me at the rate of a digit per second. My personal best for memorizing a deck of 52 shuffled cards is 28.5 seconds. (Andi Bell holds the official world record at 34.01 seconds.) One of my goals is to regain the record for the most random decimal numbers memorized in 5 minutes – my unrecorded personal best stands at 336.

CHAPTER ONE

A BRIEF HISTORY OF MEMORY

From ancient times to the modern age

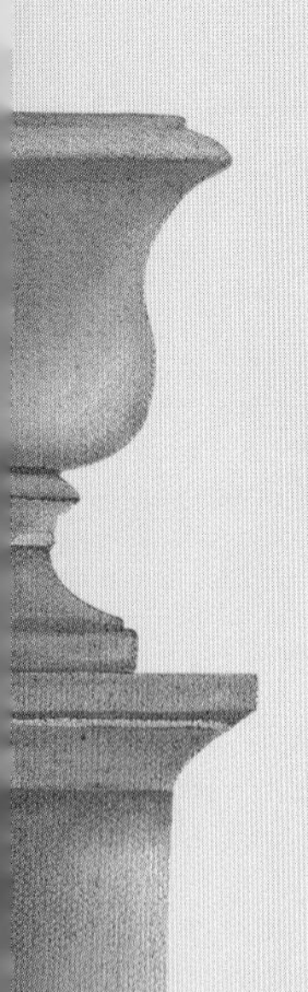

We may regard memory as one of humankind's oldest arts. To our ancient ancestors, it was not just a useful aid to survival, but an integral part of daily life. In the absence of the printing press, memory was the slate on which history was recorded. This was how we sorted information to help us make sense of the world. Reference devices were more primitive as well as thinner on the ground, so if facts and figures were to be at the fingertips of the ancients, they had to be remembered – a job for intellect and imagination. Throughout this early period of history, a good memory was a prerequisite for success: epic poets, notably Homer, memorized their works long before they were ever written down; and politicians, theologians and philosophers persuaded their audiences by delivering effective and convincing speeches, the memory cues for which were visualized colourfully in their heads. In this chapter we look at how memory has been used and understood through the ages.

Oral Traditions

As children, and even as adults, some of the most wonderful stories we hear are those of our own ancestry – tales that have travelled along the branches of our family tree like an army of determined ants. With each retelling, slight changes may be introduced – perhaps an embellishment or exaggeration to hold the wandering attention of a restless young listener, or an invention or two to bridge an awkward gap in the known facts. This is how memories are polished to make them smoother and easier to pass on to others. Yet the basic body of information usually remains broadly intact. By listening to dozens of stories, we accumulate a knowledge of our past. We may look at old family photographs, but without the context that memories – whether first- or second-hand – supply, such physical records are merely visual ciphers.

If we go way back in time, before the invention of the personal organizer, before we had diaries or even writing, we revisit an age when oral tradition was the only method of passing memories from one generation to the next. Anything not recounted for the benefit of others would disappear from the collective consciousness, forgotten for ever. Hence, enormous importance was placed upon memory among the ancients – it was recognized that without memory and reminiscence the cultural heritage would be lost. There were a few libraries in ancient Athens, and there was also a limited book trade, but these were no substitute for a wise man with a good memory.

We all have a vague image of the great epic poet Homer, whose feats of oral storytelling were no less heroic than the Greek and Trojan warriors whose stories he told. Homer no doubt relied on certain well-worn poetic formulae, improvised around a body of familiar material, and may even have used writing as an ancillary aid, at least for the *Iliad*, which consisted of 16,000 verses and would have taken four or five long evenings to recite. Yet there is no doubt that a spectacular ability to memorize lay at the heart of his skills as a performer.

Homer's great epics would have been somewhat fluid until in due course they were committed to writing. By contrast, in the Vedic tradition of ancient India it was believed that any inaccuracies in the chanting of any of the sacred hymns of the *Rigveda* would cause an imbalance in the cosmos, with dire consequences for humankind. In order to avoid such a catastrophe, Vedic priests carefully honed their memories so as never to make a mistake, and this has resulted in a highly unusual phenomenon: a scripture, born out of oral tradition, that is believed to be very close to its original, spoken form.

Storytelling is a natural way to spend long winter nights in a village, which is one explanation, as we pass into the Middle Ages, for the myths of northern Europe – extended tales of gods, giants, dragons and strange transformations, whose origins are lost to us but certainly belong to an oral tradition. The extreme nature of the subject matter, with its grotesque and magical episodes, made it perfect for memorization – an obvious link between the surreal and the memorable that operates in the most effective memory systems today. After all, what could be more vivid than Ragnarok, the last great apocalyptic battle between gods and giants which in the mythology of the Norsemen marks the ending of the world? Once heard, such tales could scarcely be forgotten.

The Ancient Greeks

Mnemonic – the word we use for a device that aids the memory – is related to the name Mnemosyne, the Greek goddess of memory, who was said to have known everything that is past, present and future. She was believed to be the basis of all life and creativity (an association derived from her role as the mother of the Nine Muses, who were the inspiration for all aspects of literature, science and the arts). Moreover, myth tells us that if a mortal were to drink from Lethe, the river of Death, all his or her memories would be lost for ever. From these mythic associations we can deduce that for the ancient Greeks memory was the fount of inspiration, and that its loss was synonymous with death – making it a faculty to be held in the highest esteem.

The so-called "father" of memory training was Simonides of Ceos, a Greek lyric poet who lived during the mid 5th–6th centuries BCE. Having delivered a speech at a banquet, Simonides was summoned with a message that two men were waiting outside to see him. As soon as Simonides emerged from the building, the structure collapsed, crushing everyone inside to death. (The two men never appeared, but were said to have been the twin gods Castor and Pollux, who saved Simonides because he had praised them in his speech.) The bodies were too damaged for the families to identify, but by thinking back to where each guest had been seated during the banquet Simonides determined who was who.

In one stroke, Simonides had demonstrated his first principle of memory – that of *locus*, or place. By attaching images of what we need to remember to specific places, such as the rooms of a house or the chairs around a dinner table, we impose a logical structure on a group of items that are otherwise unrelated, thus making them easier to recall. To remember any sequence of data (be they names, a shopping list or points in a speech), a practitioner of the locus technique would mentally retrace their steps through the place in which they imagined the information had been stored. (Interestingly, the English word "topic", meaning a subject or theme, is derived from the Greek *topos*, a place.)

Although the Greek texts on memory are believed to have been lost long ago, the techniques they taught are preserved in Latin texts written between the 1st century BCE and the 1st century CE (see p.18). From these we find that the Greeks established and developed many guidelines to ensure the reliable operation of their locus method. For example, they devised the idea that the locus should be somewhere familiar to the memorizer, and that people and actions should be used as much as possible to make any visualizations deposited in the locus more memorable. They believed that the senses had a strong role to play in memorization, especially sight. And the philosopher Aristotle is said to have recognized the importance of association – making connections in the mind, which enable us to take short, logical steps when storing and retrieving a memory. We will come across all these ideas later in this book – because each of them remains relevant to memory enhancement today.

A great and beautiful invention is memory, always useful both for learning and for life.

Dialexeis
400BCE

The Ancient Romans

The ancient Romans, like the Greeks before them, attributed prime importance to memory skills. Citizens were greatly impressed by the memorization feats displayed by trained orators, and were quick to see its value in the political theatre of the times. They believed that memorization was a fundamental component of rhetoric – without memorizing the structure of a speech, how could an orator make an impassioned plea or convincing argument?

Perhaps the most famous Roman to write about memory was the great politician and orator Marcus Cicero (106–43BCE), who helped to bring Greek teachings on memory to the Latin world in his work *De Oratore* ("On Rhetoric"). Quintilian (*c*.35–*c*.95CE), too, wrote an influential work called the *Institutio Oratoria* ("The Fundamentals of Rhetoric"), in which he applies the principles of the locus (see p.16) to a Roman villa. However, the most complete record of classical memory techniques appears in the *Ad Herennium* (*c*.85BCE), which predates the Cicero and Quintilian texts – it is said to have been written by a young (unnamed) boy. The techniques described in all three works draw largely upon those of the Greeks, but the *Ad Herennium* makes a unique, important distinction about types of memory, which both Cicero and Quintilian maintained: each of us has natural memory (our innate ability to memorize) but this can be improved through artificial memory – that is, memory techniques. According to Cicero, we all require our own individual levels of help from artificial memory. He himself had a good natural memory and could orate non-stop for three hours at a time, but he modestly claimed that even his memory had to be supplemented by artifice.

We should never have realized how great is the power [of memory], nor how divine it is, but for the fact that it is memory which has brought oratory to its present position of glory.

Quintilian
c.90CE

Memory's Changing Fortunes

During the Middle Ages a new perception emerged of the benefits of learning memory skills. The scholastics (medieval academics) adapted classical memory techniques to teach religion and ethics. The missionary Matteo Ricci used memory training as a vehicle to teach Christianity to the Chinese. Closer to home, the purpose of remembering the past was to inspire prudent conduct in the present and future. In addition, imagery was seen as important in bringing to life the vices and virtues – many of the preachers used vivid details during their sermons. These images were easy to lodge in the

Giulio Camillo's Memory Theatre

During the 16th century the Italian philosopher Giulio Camillo achieved great fame for his memory theatres, the purpose of which were to awaken the mind to the memory of lost divinity. Instead of simply describing an imaginary theatre, he conceived, designed and built actual, wooden ones and exhibited them throughout Italy and France, where they stimulated great interest.

Each theatre was large enough for two people to stand on its central stage, and the audience chambers were filled with ornate columns and statues of the gods, to represent "all that the mind can conceive and all that is hidden in the soul". Camillo claimed that a speech worthy of Cicero could be memorized by mentally placing its key points on the statues and columns in the theatre.

minds of listeners, to keep the hope of heaven, the fear of hell and the lessons of the Church uppermost in people's minds.

During the Renaissance, with its resurgence of interest in classical traditions and its general spirit of humanistic inquiry, there was a blossoming of interest in memory as well as the arts and science. Memory techniques were no longer the sole province of religion – in fact, the pendulum had swung back, and some people even considered these methods to be the Devil's own work. Memory theorists such as Guilio Camillo (1480–1544) and Giordano Bruno (1548–1600) adopted Plato's theory that through memory humankind could transcend life and death and join with the divine. They believed that by using memory we could understand the mind of God and interpret the order of nature. Camillo invented a series of elaborate "memory theatres" (see box, p.19), while Bruno stated that the key to reaching the divine was in the organization of the mind and its locked memories. Bruno devised many memory systems, finally completing a series of memory wheels. These wheels were seen as microcosms of the heavens, and showed the orbits of stars and planets. On them he placed symbols of the arts, languages and sciences, and used his sensory associations to lodge images and facts related to these symbols in his mind. Then, while he observed the sky, the images he had associated with the heavens would be committed to memory and the brain would make order of the world. Branded a heretic, Bruno was burned at the stake in 1600.

In the ensuing centuries, as scientific endeavour rose to prominence, the art of memory no longer commanded such intense interest, yet the use of memory techniques never fully disappeared. In the eighteenth century, the Age of Reason, people sought to understand how the world worked. The emphasis was on discovering the

harmonious system that lay behind nature and human mind. The study of memory became part of a general investigation into biological science. People concentrated on discovering how the brain retained memories. This scientific preoccupation meant that memory techniques involving creativity were largely rejected – and the idea that a good memory was a mark of brilliance began to falter.

In the nineteenth century, memory was seen not so much as a mysterious and spiritual phenomenon but as an empty vessel that could be filled by mechanical learning and repetition of facts. This is the view behind the popular image of the Victorian schoolmaster, driving facts into his pupils' minds by hammer blows of repetition. Rote learning became the basis of educational systems (and, to some extent, still remains an important factor in schools today). This reflected an ethic of hard work, an unwillingness to believe in short-cuts, and, in the great age of scientific and industrial advance, a profound suspicion of the imagination.

Children learning geography might be able to tell the names of every known tribe in Africa or every petty island in the Pacific, without knowing the name or course of the river which ran through their respective towns.

An English school inspector's report 1846

Memory in Modern Times

The twentieth century has seen a shift in the study of memory. Instead of looking for ways to improve our memories (for example, to build skills that will further our politicial ambitions), scientific advances have taken us toward a better understanding of how memories are formed and stored in the brain. One of the most remarkable memory studies was undertaken by the Russian psychologist Alexander Luria between 1920 and 1950. His subject was a journalist named Shereshevsky, known simply as "S", who confounded his colleagues by never taking notes at editorial meetings. He did not need to: he could remember every word, name, date and telephone number that he was told. As Luria tested S with increasingly complex data, all of which S could remember years later, it transpired that S accomplished his amazing feats by translating everything he heard into strong mental images or sensual experiences. But S was not doing this purposely – he had a condition called synesthesia, in which the boundaries of the senses sporadically become blurred, so that he might read the word "door" and experience a salty taste or see the colour red. The condition goes some way to proving how using the senses during memorization can create a series of imaginative pegs on which to hang pieces of information.

Since S's time, psychologists have studied many hundreds of other subjects, some with unusual memory defects or abilities, most with normal memory function and capacity. Their research has yielded several theories on the way in which memory works. Although many aspects of memory's physiology remain a mystery, we are increasingly aware of how well designed were the techniques used by the ancient Greeks and Romans – how well adapted to the functioning of the human brain.

Recently, perhaps the most influential development in memory has occurred not in the human mind but in machines. Our memory skills have become neglected as we increasingly rely upon external means of recording information – from the video to the personal organizer. We rate our computers by the size of their "memory" and the speed with which they access it. We marvel at the versatility of the internet. Yet we neglect to realize the full potential that our own brains possess. Memory skills are not taught in schools, yet memory is still tested in examinations. Most people do not know that memory can be extended by techniques anyone can master. We must look back to the ancients and revive their faith in the mind.

The Memory Chip

The computer analogy is often used to explain the workings of memory. But is this really accurate? One distinction between human and computer memory is the relative ability of each to evaluate information. Once a computer has stored data, so long as it is given the appropriate retrieval cues, the computer will bring back that information perfectly in its most recently inputted form. In human memory, the information that we store and retrieve is subjective – it is susceptible to mood, opinion, upbringing, and a host of other social factors.

One other difference between computer and human memory is our ability to remember layers of data in the same mental "document". In a computer's memory, of course, once data is overwritten, that information is lost for ever.

CHAPTER TWO

THE MEMORY MAZE

How memory works

In the 4th century BCE, the Greek philosopher Plato alleged that memories were etched on our brains like the scratches of a pointed stick in wax. Eventually, each etching would be worn away and replaced by something new. The delightful simplicity of this theory belies the intensely intricate brain functions that enable us to memorize, retain and recall. Despite vigorous scientific research during the last hundred years, memory remains a mysterious, awe-inspiring phenomenon – a wonderful maze in which surprising self-discoveries lie in wait for us if we are prepared to stretch our minds to realize more of their potential. In this chapter we look at the basic physiology and psychology of memory in the context of the brain as a whole. Of course, we do not need to know how electricity works to be able to switch on a light. But learning something of the science awakens us to the miraculous gift of memory, for which we should all be thankful.

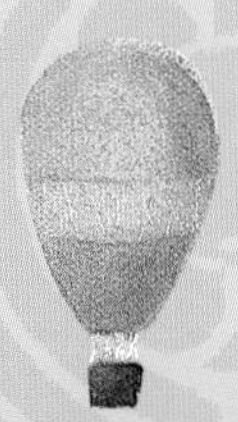

The Landscape of the Mind

Memory has always been vital to our survival. Early nomadic humans needed to remember where sources of game, nuts and berries were plentiful, and where they could find shelter in winter. Perhaps most importantly, they needed to be able to recognize faces to determine whether an approaching figure was a friend or foe. Our memory has evolved alongside other facets of our intelligence and the brain itself. Although the brain is an extremely complex structure, a simplified overview of some of its regions and functions can provide a useful background to how our memory works.

The average adult brain weighs between 1,000 and 1,500 grams (2–3lb) and has the consistency of a soft-boiled egg. It serves as a command post and the processing centre for our primary physical and cognitive functions, including movement, speech, thought and perception. It is also the powerhouse of memory.

The lower part of the brain contains the *brain stem*, connecting the brain to the spinal cord. Attached to the brain stem is the *cerebellum*, which controls the body's movements. Above the brain stem is the *thalamus*, containing the limbic system – thought to affect our motivation and emotions. Just below the thalamus is the *hypothalamus*, a pea-sized region, which maintains the body's temperature and chemical make-up; it also helps control sleep and the emotions. Collectively, the thalamus and the hypothalamus are known as the *midbrain*. The higher, more complex functions of the brain (the ones that make us uniquely human), take place in the upper region of the brain: the *cerebrum*. Memory, language and creativity are some of these higher functions.

The *cerebral cortex*, the layer of the brain that covers the *cerebrum*, is the most important region as far as memory is concerned. The cortex is large and covered with furrows and ridges, which greatly increase its surface area so that it can hold a greater number of cells. Although the cortex comprises only 25 per cent of the brain's total volume, it contains 75 per cent of the brain cells – known as *neurons*. Primarily involved in integrating and processing sensory information, the cortex contains two large regions called the *frontal lobes*, which are believed to help us store and recall memories. The lobes are also associated with our emotions, personality and intelligence.

Altogether, the brain consists of some 10 billion neurons. Each neuron reaches out to one or more other neurons using minute fibres known as *axons* and *dendrites* every time we undertake any sort of mental activity. There are recognizable groups of neurons in the brain, but in principle a neuron can communicate with any other brain cell to form a thought or memory, or to precipitate a course of action. Every time we use our brain to make a memory, certain neurons transmit electrical impulses at lightning speed along their axons. The impulses are picked up by the dendrites of other cells – forming a type of electrical circuitry in the brain.

Each neuron may have hundreds of dendrites. Between each dendrite and each fibre at the end of the receiving cell's axon is a tiny gap, known as a *synapse*. When we use our brains, the electrical impulses sent along the axons cause messenger chemicals, called *neurotransmitters*, to be released by the axon of one neuron and flow across the synapse to the dendrite of the adjacent neuron. Different types of neurotransmitter carry different types of message – for example, *serotonin* acts as a natural painkiller and *dopamine* inhibits some of our movements. In addition, there are two types of synapse: *excitatory synapses*, which stimulate an electrical impulse in the next neuron, and *inhibitory synapses*, which prevent the electrical impulse from taking place. Together they control the unceasing activity of the brain, which is firing billions of impulses at any given moment. The action of the synapses in regulating brain activity is largely responsible for how we encode our memories.

As for the brain,
it is all mystery
and memory
and electricity.

Richard Selzer
b.1928

Membranes called *meninges* protect the brain. They are surrounded by the cerebrospinal fluid, which cushions the brain against the skull, and they also supply the brain with oxygen and nutrients. Our brains need a constant supply of proteins, enzymes, salts and other molecules such as glucose and calcium ions to manufacture the neurotransmitters, to enable the axons and dendrites to extend toward each other and for memories to be laid down. The brain's constant functioning means that it requires a great deal of oxygen to keep the neurons alive. The brain claims only three per cent of the body's weight, but it uses 20 per cent of our oxygen intake.

Catching the "Jizz"

EXERCISE ONE

We recognize people in an instant, without having to think about the distinguishing features that make such recognition possible. Birdwatchers identify birds from a distance in a similar way, by what they term "jizz" (adapted from General Impression by Shape and Size). Human "jizz" may comprise not only the obvious components of the face, but also more subtle characteristics, such as a walking with a slight hunch, a flick of the head, the ways the hands hang from an undersized jacket. This exercise is designed to show how the slightest clues clinch recognition, in a way that demonstrates the extraordinary power of the brain as a processing tool.

1. As you walk around your local neighbourhood, look for people you know by sight. Scan around you, and look at quite distant figures. You are certain to pick out familiar figures – even if you are not actually acquainted with them.

2. Itemize the features that make such figures recognizable. What is the farthest distance over which you can make a confident identification? You may be surprised at your powers of recognition – which are dependent on memories stored unconsciously in the brain.

Left Brain, Right Brain

The cerebrum or upper part of the brain – where memories and skills, such as language, are situated – is divided into two hemispheres, the left and right. The left brain controls the right side of the body, while the right brain controls the left side, although no-one can explain why this is so. A thick network of fibres, called the *corpus callosum*, bridges the gap between the halves, allowing them to communicate with each other. If this bridge is destroyed, the subject's awareness of the body is totally divided – so, the left brain continues to process the experiences of the right side of the body, but the right brain has no knowledge of the actions, experiences or sensations of that side at all; and vice versa.

Scientists once believed that the left and right brains governed different mental functions. But a more accurate view is that each hemisphere processes information in a different way. In most people, the left brain is more specialized in "serial processing" – analyzing information in a linear fashion, one piece after another. This makes it ideal for hearing and remembering speech, as well as processing numerical information, and logical problem-solving. The right brain excels at "parallel processing" – synthesizing several pieces of information at one time into a coherent whole. It is better suited for recognizing and remembering pictures, physical features and emotions. Some say that the left side of the brain is the analyst and the right side the aesthete. Epileptics who, in the 1960s, had operations to sever the corpus callosum subsequently "forgot" how to write with their left hands and how to draw with their right (just as we would expect: each hand is controlled by the opposite hemisphere).

However, the distinction is not clear cut: the left brain *can* work as a parallel processor if it needs to, and the right brain *is* capable of linear analysis. Nevertheless, specialization of the two hemispheres begins early in life and seems to be genetically pre-programmed. Measurements of electrical activity in the brains of newborn babies show that the left brain responds to a click and the right to a flash of light. In addition, the level of logical/creative activity in each hemisphere varies between the genders. Women's brains tend to be more flexible than men's – if a woman's left hemisphere is damaged, she loses less of her verbal ability.

To use our brain, and therefore our memory, to maximum capacity, we need to engage both sides of the brain in all we think and do. Most of the time we manage this naturally. For example, if we play a musical instrument, our appreciation of the music takes place in our right brain but recollecting the tune and the actions required to play the instrument takes place in the left brain. Musicians who have suffered injuries to their left hemisphere can still appreciate music, even though they have lost their ability to compose, play an instrument or sing in key.

In order to improve our memory, we need consciously to engage both hemispheres of the brain at all stages of memorization and retrieval: when we take in new information; when we store it in our brain (thus creating a memory); and when we attempt the processes of recall necessary to bring the information back into our consciousness. All of the memory techniques in this book follow the principle that both logic and creativity must be employed if a memory is to make a lasting impression upon our brain. Only then is the stage perfectly set for optimum recall.

Waves of Memory

The brain is continually active, even while we sleep. During the chemical processes that create memories, as well as those that conduct our other mental functions, the neurons of the brain spontaneously fire impulses at varying intervals, to create charges of electrical activity that fluctuate in voltage. The different frequencies of this electrical activity are known as *brain waves*.

Scientific investigation into the brain has determined that we produce different types of brain wave according to our various activities and thoughts. The beta rhythm is the normal rhythm of the brain when we are awake and active. The speed of the beta rhythm varies according to our levels of activity and how stressed we feel (when we are stressed we emit a fast beta rhythm). When we are awake, but resting with our eyes closed, our brain waves flow in the alpha rhythm. Sometimes we produce two or more different brain-wave rhythms at the same time. For example, when we are in a deep sleep we produce a mixture of theta rhythms (which are slower than alpha rhythms) and delta rhythms (the slowest of all). During dreaming, or when we are drowsy (halfway between sleeping and waking), we produce only theta rhythms.

In order to optimize our ability to memorize, retain and recall information, we need to make the most of our brain when it is highly suggestive – that is, when it is emitting theta rhythms (preferably combined with alpha rhythms). But, since we are unable to memorize as we sleep, what does this mean in a practical sense? If we can find a way to encourage our brain to emit theta and alpha brain waves during consciousness, we will put ourselves in the correct

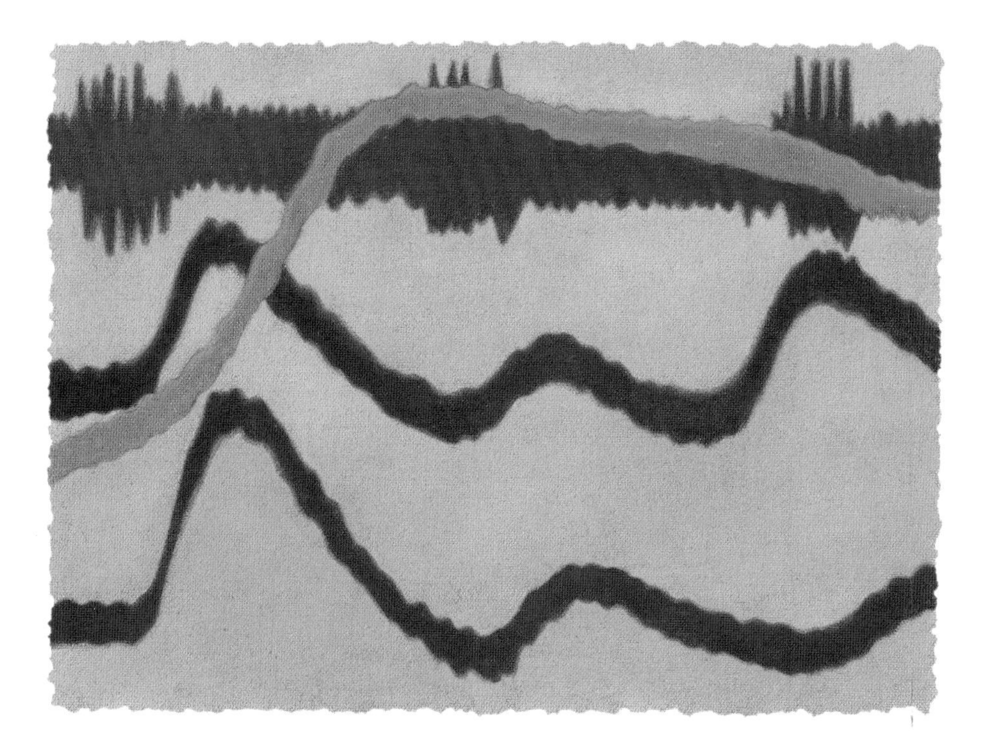

"frame of mind" for optimum memorization. To do this, all we need to do is learn to relax. For many years, I have been practising meditation, which has not only benefitted my emotional well-being, but has also enabled me to train myself to slow down my brain waves so that I can memorize effectively. One of the easiest meditation exercises is a focus on the breath – try it every day for ten minutes to get yourself used to mental relaxation. Close your eyes and draw air up through your nostrils and into your lungs, in one long, slow inhalation. Breathe out through your nose: mentally focus on the air flowing out through the right nostril. Breathe in again, and on the outbreath focus on the left nostril. Alternate your focus during the exercise. When you come to memorize, try to recreate and tap into the calm (the theta waves) you experience during meditation.

Types of Memory

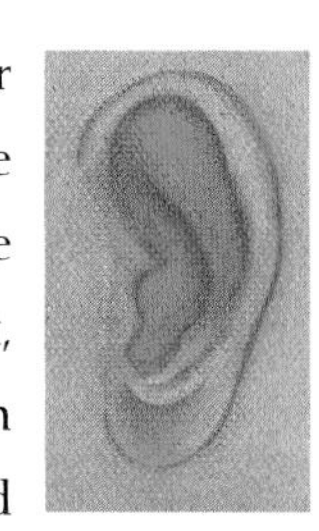

We use our memory constantly – each new thought or experience triggers a host of existing memory traces in the brain, whether or not we are consciously aware of them. Once awakened, they interact with the new stimulus, interpreting it, classifying it and often altering it – however subtly – to fit in with what they "know" to be true. The sight of a red-capped fungus in the woods might conjure up the flavour of wild mushrooms, along with childhood warnings about the dangers of eating them. We may even hear the voice of the parent who delivered the warning. At the same time, there will be a mass of other, fleeting, memories. Part of the brain might even register the mushroom shape and evoke images of atomic explosions. Part will respond to the redness, recalling blood and danger signs. Most of the memories will be so momentary that we will not notice them, but many of them will play a part in governing our actions.

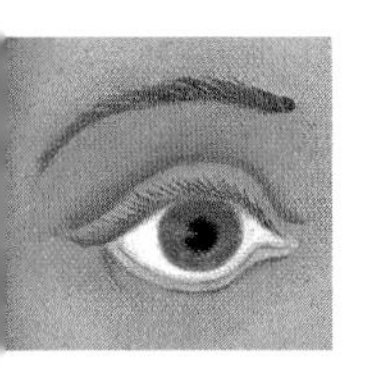

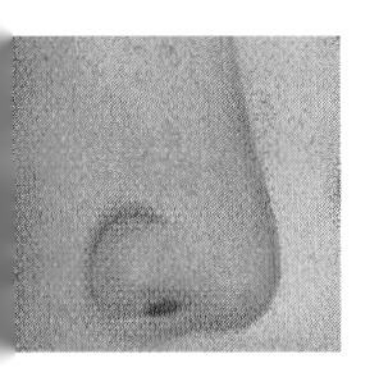

Since the nineteenth century scientists have speculated that the rich variety of our memories could be broken down into separate categories, and that each one might exist in a different region of the brain. Although their attempts to find these regions have had limited success, a few of the classifications have survived. The most important of them distinguishes between sensory memory, short-term memory (STM) and long-term memory (LTM).

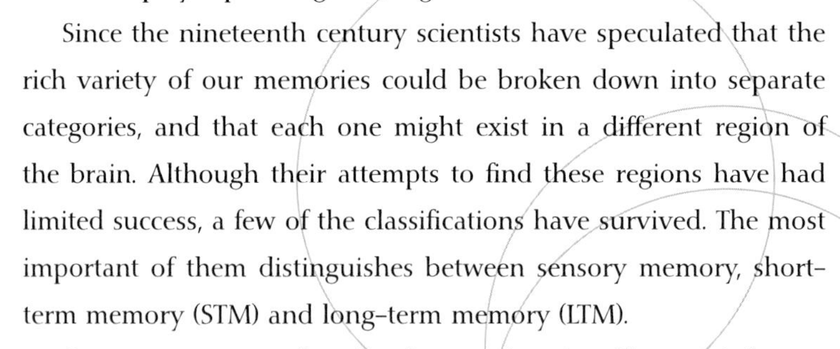

Sensory memory has the shortest duration. The raw information gathered by our senses – sight, hearing, taste, smell and touch – flows into a sensory store, which is distributed between different regions of the brain. Each sense has its own associated region, which is responsible for processing its input. For example, visual information is dealt with toward the rear of the cortex, while the primary hearing centre is in the temporal lobe (a part of the cortex at the side of the brain). There are also so-called association areas in the brain, linking the sensory regions and allowing all the different inputs to be pulled together into a coherent whole.

The amount of information that can be held by the sensory store is practically unlimited, although the sensory data generally lasts for only a fraction of a second before it is replaced by new stimuli. An image in the visual cortex – called an *icon* – lasts long enough for a modern movie, projected at 24 frames per second, to seem continuous (the image of each frame is still in the mind when the next is projected). But a silent movie, projected at its original speed of 18 frames per second, appears to flicker because the icon of each frame has already begun to fade before the next appears. Auditory information seems to last longer than data from the other senses, lingering for several seconds before it fades from our sensory memory.

The sensory store filters the signals from the senses and monitors them at an unconscious level. The vast majority of sensory information is almost immediately discarded, but a tiny percentage is selected by the monitoring procedure because it meets certain criteria – for example, an image may be intensely coloured, or fast-moving, or an overheard sentence may contain a familiar name – and is passed on to the short-term memory. This is not a simple one-step process. To the sensory memory, an apple is nothing more than a red or green, shiny, round solid. For us to perceive an apple, this information must first go to the long-term memory – also known as the permanent or reference memory – to be compared with the elements already there, in an effort to recognize what it is that we are seeing. Only after some sort of approximate match is found can

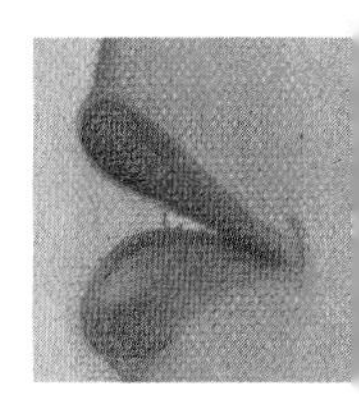

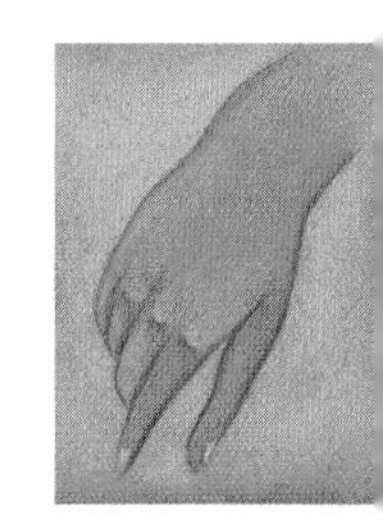

the brain create a short-term memory. The whole complicated sequence is almost instantaneous.

Short-term memory is also known as the active or working memory, because it depends on the electrochemical activity of excited neurons, and because it is often used to achieve specific tasks – such as adding up a bill. Short-term memory generally holds information for only ten to twenty seconds, but it is vital to any activity that requires conscious thought – even a simple activity such as understanding a sentence.

However, STM has a limited capacity. It can normally hold approximately seven pieces of information simultaneously (see p.51) – whether they are numbers, words or images – and any new input displaces whatever is already there. As a result, a short-term memory is easily lost because of distractions, either from outside sources or from other thoughts. Nevertheless, if such a memory is sufficiently powerful – because it is the focus of intense concentration, or is repeated over and over, or is particularly surprising or emotional – it can become a long-term memory. This happens when the neurological activity associated with STM changes the physical structure of the brain (see p.42), a change that may last anything from minutes to decades. In fact, it is possible that all long-term memories last for life, but that some of them are more difficult than others to access. The memory trace remains somewhere in the brain, but we are no longer sure how to find it.

Long-term memory was the subject of research by psychologists and computer programmers in the 1970s. A distinction was made between different types of long-term memory stored by the brain: *declarative* (or explicit) memories and *procedural* (or implicit) memories. Declarative memories allow us to name things, and to recognize what is meant by names. They are the sum of the facts and information that we have accumulated over the course of our lives. These include mundane recollections, such as what we had for dinner last night (which is unlikely to last for more than a few days), and momentous occasions, such as births and deaths (which will probably last many years). All the memories that relate to events in our own lives are called *episodic*. They are affected by the passage of time and will fade according to how rarely or how often we recall them, as well as the importance we placed upon the incidents when they happened. The more powerful an impression an event makes, the longer our memory of it will last. *Factual* memory is the name for more impersonal knowledge, such as mathematical formulae or lines from Shakespeare. *Semantic* memory is what gives meaning to all this information, so that when we remember or hear the phrase

Do Animals Remember?

The phrase to have a "memory like an elephant" means to have a good memory; while to have a "memory like a fish" means to have a bad one. But can animals truly remember? Some have highly developed genetic memory – many species (such as horses and giraffes) are able to walk from the moment of birth, an ability inherited in their genes from their parents (unlike human babies).

Much of the behaviour of wild animals is pre-programmed before birth. Unlike humans, wild animals rely upon instinctual behaviour more than learned experiences.

Contrarily, most pet owners claim that animals show signs of recognition and learning: think how the cat comes running when it hears its owners' footsteps; or how most pets respond to the call of their names.

"A rose by any other name ... " we know that a rose is a flower, that its stem is thorny, that it has an attractive perfume and is often sent as a romantic token, and so on. Although this system of classification is popular among some psychologists, others have described it as artificial, believing that it may not reflect major differences in how the brain remembers: learning a play by Shakespeare, they argue, is itself an episode in a student's life, and the lines may be stored in the same way as the memory of a birthday party.

On the other hand, some experts believe that semantic memory may well use somewhat different mental processes. It seems that our memory of rules and concepts is much less susceptible to the process of forgetting than is our memory for facts. We remember the meaning of a sentence long after we have forgotten the exact words. In one experiment, university undergraduates who were told about a Native American hunting trip in canoes later remembered the story as being about a fishing trip in boats – something with which they were more familiar. The words were misremembered in order to preserve a more expected sense. Some believe that forgetting precise facts is partly a sacrifice to preserve our semantic memory.

Procedural memory is very different from declarative memory, and seems to involve completely different parts of the nervous system. It is the memory of how to do things, rather than what they are, and it allows us to perform acquired skills – for the most part unconsciously – such as riding a bike and even walking upright. None of these abilities is acquired easily, but it is often claimed that, once in place, a procedural memory lasts a lifetime. People who have not ridden a bike in years relearn the skill in minutes. Jockeys who have been thrown from a mount and brain-damaged so badly that they are no longer able to recognize a horse, or

identify their animal when asked to do so, are still capable of riding it. For this reason it has been suggested that, whereas declarative memories exist solely in the brain, procedural memories may in part be stored throughout the body, in the nerve cells that control the muscles.

However, some researchers have discovered that the survival of procedural memory depends upon the skill concerned. Only continuous skills that require a constantly varying response to a constantly varying stimulus are remembered for a lifetime – such as riding a bike, or anything involving balance. So-called discrete skills, requiring a succession of separate actions – such as driving a car – are not nearly so permanent, and can deteriorate noticeably without practice, even after a relatively short period of time.

How Memories are Created

In order to understand how a memory is created, we need to have some idea of how the brain functions. The human brain does not work the same way as a computer – even though this has been one of the most popular analogies applied to our brains in recent years. The computer is only a serial device – it deals with one piece of data at a time, before moving on to the next. The brain, on the other hand, can also act as a "parallel processor", handling many pieces of information simultaneously, and forging links between the items in as it does so. A computer memory keeps data in a precise location, tagged for easy retrieval; while the brain appears to store memories in a less systematic way – the same memory can, in theory at least, be retrieved from many different parts of the brain and by many different routes. Some memories may not be accessible at all, because they have been eccentrically labelled during storage and we do not know how to find them. For example, I may have a clear memory of blowing out the candles on my fourth-birthday cake, but no idea whatsoever who else was in the room as I did so. One possible explanation for this is that my memory of the guests has not been "filed" under birthday party, but under some other, unexpected, heading, such as "people who have stared at me".

However, in some ways the computer analogy is a helpful one. A memory is stored as a result of electrical signals causing a change in the physical structure of the brain, and similar electrical signals are involved in the recovery of that memory. The moment we perceive – or recollect – anything, a short-term memory of it is created (or re-created) in the form of a complicated sequence of electro-

chemical impulses that are passed back and forth among a network of neurons in the brain. The enormously complex pattern of this network, and the varying frequencies at which the neurons pulse, play a major part in "encoding" the memory. Indeed, the pattern in the network of neurons does not just represent the memory, it *is* – literally – the memory. Far from being simply an elaborate cipher experienced by the conscious mind, the pattern is an active ingredient of consciousness (which, according to modern neuroscience, is only the sum of all the electrical activity that occurs in the brain).

This process of apparent encoding is only possible because the brain is so complex. The brain has billions of neurons, dendrites and synapses. The activity of a single neuron could set off a cascade of impulses that can theoretically course through the brain along more different pathways than there are atoms in the universe.

The interactions between the neurons in a new short-term memory create a pattern, or *trace*, that is quickly lost unless it is consolidated into a long-term memory. Many different factors affect how likely it is that a short-term memory will be consolidated – for example, whether we are particularly stressed or distracted. The process by which memory is consolidated appears to involve the thalamus and a region near the centre of the brain called the *hippocampus*, which we can think of as providing energy for the creation of long-term memories in other parts of the brain.

Memory consolidation relies upon the plasticity of the brain – the way that it is continuously modifying itself. We have already seen that an active memory is a pattern of electrical impulses passing around a group of neurons. Making long-term memories involves changing the physical characteristics of the brain – including increasing the number of synapses along the desired route – so that some patterns are more easily activated, or excited, than others. The easier a pattern is to generate and regenerate, the more easily the associated memories are created and recalled.

When a neurotransmitter is passed across a synapse, it does not just stimulate an electrical signal in the dendrite. It also stimulates the production of *ribonucleic acid* (RNA), which, among other things, controls the manufacture of proteins in the brain cell. Recent research has led scientists to believe that the proteins that are synthesized in the cell are used to build extra and larger synapses on the excited dendrites, thereby making the dendrites even easier to excite in future (thus consolidating that particular memory). The physical memory traces created through such permanent changes in the brain's structure are sometimes known as *engrams*.

Finding Your Digit Span

EXERCISE TWO

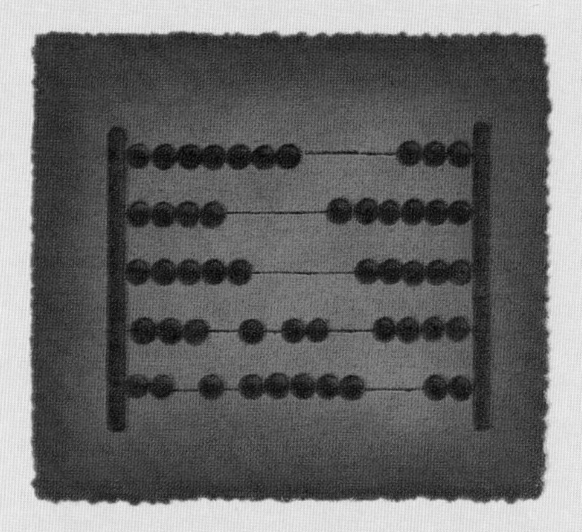

This exercise will reveal how much data you are able to hold in your short-term memory (STM) before it is replaced. Choose the required sequences of random single-digit numbers from a telephone directory.

1. On a large sheet of paper write down a sequence of four numbers on the top line, such as 5, 8, 3, 7. Write two more sequences of four digits below. On the fourth, fifth and sixth lines write sequences of five digits. On the next three lines write sequences of six digits, and continue until you have sequences of 10 digits on the bottom three lines.

2. Now read the number sequence on the first line to yourself at a steady pace. Then conceal that sequence by covering it with another piece of paper and try to recall the numbers in the same order. Move the cover sheet away and note whether or not you remembered the numbers completely correctly. If so, move on to the first sequence of the next length. If not, try the next sequence of the same length.

3. Continue testing yourself until you reach a sequence length at which you cannot correctly repeat the numbers on any of the three attempts. Your digit span is the number of digits contained in the longest sequence of numbers that you are able to recall.

The Reliability of Memory

Our memories are a unique, highly personal faculty – just as our minds are generally. All experience is subjective, and different people will recall the same experience differently (sometimes significantly so). However, this does not necessarily mean that one person's memory is better than another's. More likely, we colour our experiences with our own set of personal preoccupations – our likes and dislikes, our mood at the time, and so on. Does this mean, then, that we cannot trust our memories reliably to present the facts about a situation or experience? Should we be sceptical about what our memories insist really happened? If we feel convinced that we have the answer to a searching question, can we really trust the depth of our conviction?

The memory represents to us not what we choose but what it pleases.

Montaigne
1580–58

These questions suggest themselves most challengingly within the deeper realms of psychology, where various mechanisms of the mind may distort our recollection of events. For example, we may transfer our own sense of guilt onto other people and, in the light of our negative feelings about these people, our memories may exaggerate incidents that show them in a bad light. Or we may suppress what is painful about the past – perhaps an uncomfortable incident from childhood or adolescence. A commonplace example of our mind's anesthetizing process centres on childbirth. At the time of labour, women live through the experience as painful and distressing. But if mothers are asked later to recount their memory of childbirth, most will say that they "know" instinctively that it was painful at the time, but that they cannot recapture in any detail the intensity or difficulty of the event. (This is the product of a simple survival instinct, which ensures that, on the whole, women are not deterred from having more children.)

At a more obvious level, stress in the form of tiredness, fear or ill-health can have a significant effect on what we take in and how accurately we can recall it. When we are under pressure of any kind, our ability to concentrate lessens, and we become less capable of faithfully observing details. This is a particular problem when eyewitnesses to an accident or crime are asked to give evidence. The accuracy of this type of information has been the subject of many psychological studies. Despite the fact that we often assume the opposite to be true, psychologist Elizabeth Loftus found that scenes of violence or damage, whether real or fictitious (for example, in a movie), are actually less clearly and accurately remembered than

Flashbulb Memories

Do you remember what you were doing when you heard of Princess Diana's death (August 31, 1997)? When a very shocking event takes place, often we recall a host of trivial details that occurred in our lives at the same time, such as where we were or who we were with. These are called flashbulb memories. Psychologists James Kulick and Roger Brown, who identified this phenomenon in 1977, proposed that a shocking event may activate a special process in the brain, which they called a "now print". Unlike normal memory, this "freezes" the moment in the mind, like a snapshot. Insignificant details, such as the quality of the light, may be remembered with hyperclarity. Flashbulb memories are not immune to distortion, but many are extremely accurate and persist longer than ordinary memories.

non-violent scenes. During times of stress it is important that you give your memory a chance – treat it sympathetically, as you would a person who has been subjected to shock. Try to seek perspectives from other people before deciding on a course of action. Do not make decisions hastily. At such times you may find yourself relying more than usual on written notes, as a back-up to memory. Once the time of stress has passed, your confidence in your memory's powers will return to its former strength.

In small doses, stress may help us to draw information from our mind. For example, during an examination, adrenaline may help us to narrow our focus on key issues. However, when stress makes us fearful, we are more likely to lose concentration, miss details or even lose touch with important memories entirely.

Another factor in the reliability of our memory concerns the associations that we make, whether consciously or unconsciously, when storing a memory. Many scientists believe that a memory acquires something of the characteristics of the older, more firmly established memories to which it is attached. Thus, the primary information or experience is distorted slightly when it is stored. In clinical tests, people were asked to memorize nonsense images, including a jagged shape that was reminiscent of the outline of a five-pointed star. The participants were assumed to fix the memory of the jagged shape in their minds by mentally attaching it to a star shape. When asked to recall the image, they could remember that the true star shape was not quite right, but they did not have a distinct memory of the jagged shape. The theory is that when we come across something that does not seem to have a frame of reference in our experience to date, we attach it to something similar, and so in recall the memory of the information or experience becomes skewed.

Hosting a Memory Forum

EXERCISE THREE

Try this exercise with a group of friends or family. The aim is to gain a complete recollection of an event by pooling everyone's memories. Make sure the forum is fun, not formal – laughter will help everyone's recall.

1. Gather together a group of people who have all been present at the same event. Perhaps you might choose a picnic with relatives (including children for an extra dimension); or a dinner party with some close friends. You might like to include memory triggers in your gathering – for example, the same food or background music as at the original event.

2. Tell your guests which occasion they will be called upon to remember only when they arrive for the forum. Spend ten to fifteen minutes together quietly trying to recall the event in as much detail as possible, each individual making notes on paper. What were people wearing? What were the topics of conversation? Did anything unexpected happen?

3. Take it in turns to offer one memory of the event at a time. Are your memories similar or widely different? If someone recalls something you do not, does this trigger a forgotten memory for you? Continue going round until the pool of memories is exhausted.

Sleep, Dreams and Memory

Many experts hold that sleep plays an important role in the consolidation of memory. The theory goes that during sleep the brain is relieved from handling the constant barrage of external stimuli with which it is bombarded during waking hours. While we are asleep, our minds are free to review, organize and file the experiences of the day.

In the drowsy dark cave of the mind/dreams build their nest with fragments/ dropped from the day's caravan.

Rabindranath Tagore 1928

There are five stages of sleep: consciousness, drowsiness, light sleep, deep sleep and dreaming sleep. During periods of dreaming sleep we experience Rapid Eye Movement (REM): our eyes flutter back and forth beneath our eyelids, and dreams are particularly frequent and vivid. Several times during the night we drift down through the five levels and up again – the periods of dreaming (or REM) sleep gradually increasing in frequency and length. During REM our heart rate increases and our brain waves are of a similar frequency to the ones that occur during consciousness (see pp.32–3). Research that was carried out during the 1960s showed that people who were deprived of REM sleep suffered memory impairment when they were awake. From this we know that REM sleep is important for the consolidation of memories.

One theory about the link between sleep and memory function is that REM sleep stimulates the activity of the hippocampus (see p.42), which, during sleep, replays certain activities or experiences of the day throughout the brain's cortex (where memories are formed and stored). This further impresses the memory traces on the brain, making them easier to recollect when we are awake.

The theory that REM sleep aids our memory is further supported by the fact that if we have spent a large part of the day learning new information, our need for sleep increases. Studies have shown that the type of sleep that makes up this requirement is REM sleep.

Although we cannot be entirely sure of the correlations between REM sleep and remembering, evidence does suggest that dreams are important for a good memory. Our periods of dreamful sleep often reveal that we remember much more of waking life than we think we do. Try searching your dreams for clues that might be references to your past. Could a child in last night's dream have symbolized a younger you? Were any dreams set in places known to you in the past, but that you no longer visit? Scouring your dreams in this way can often prove revealing.

A Good Night's Sleep

People often ask me what I do to prepare for a memory competition. I exercise my brain through memorization practice; and I make sure that my circulation is at its best through physical exercise. But, just as importantly, immediately before competing, I make sure that I have a good night's sleep.

First, in the afternoon of the day prior to a contest, I run at least four miles – which means that, once the adrenaline rush of the run has faded, I am physically tired. Second, I take some ginkgo biloba – although it has no direct relationship to improved sleep, it has been found to improve the memory. And third, I practise a presleep meditation, to quieten my anxieties about the following day (even World Champions get nervous), and to put me in the frame of mind for deep sleep.

Memory and Learning

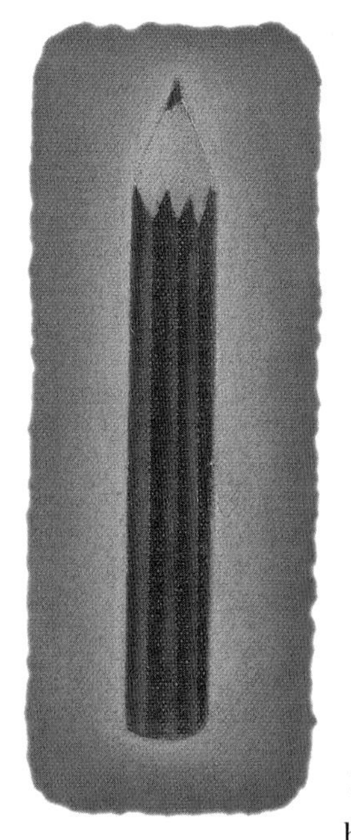

There can be no learning without memory. A wealth of psychological research has shown that for both animals and humans memory forms a crucial part of the learning process. Even the acquisition of apparently basic skills, such as when a baby learns to crawl, would be impossible without the existence of procedural (or implicit) memory.

In the early nineteenth century, the German philosopher Hermann Ebbinghaus demonstrated that the amount of information we retain depends upon the amount of time we spend learning (the "total-time hypothesis"). He also realized that it is more effective to break up the total learning time into short periods (of between fifteen and forty-five minutes), separated by five- or ten-minute breaks. This is the "distribution-practice effect", and it works partly because of a phenomenon called *reminiscence* – the way in which our memory of something actually improves steadily over a period of several minutes after we have stopped learning it. Reminiscence is probably a result of the memory traces gradually strengthening. The timescale for reminiscence varies with the type of learning: somewhat surprisingly, perhaps, our memory of a photograph is strongest one and a half minutes after studying it, while our memory of a manual skill is strongest around ten minutes after first practising it. Distributed learning increases our number of reminiscence periods. Also, when we learn blocks of information, the memories that we create interfere with each other, and regular intervals of rest lessen this effect.

Another learning strategy, applied unconsciously, is *chunking*. In 1956 American psychologist George Miller noted that the short-term memory seems able to hold only about seven items at a time, placing an upper limit on the powers of retention – if we look at a scattering of marbles on the floor, we will only be able to hold in our minds the positions of a maximum of seven of them before we become confused. Miller speculated that the short-term memory can hold vast amounts of information, provided that information is organized into no more than seven coherent "chunks". The brain seems to do this automatically – for example, as children, we did not learn the alphabet as an unbroken string of 26 letters, but used rhythm and inflection to divide it into something similar to abcd/efg/hijk/lmnop/qrs/tuv/wxyz – seven manageable units.

Memory and Intelligence

It is a common and misguided belief that we fall into two categories of intelligence – we are either bright or dim. Like many people, I did not excel at school. What is more I accepted the judgment of my teachers that I lacked potential – I knew my place and did not try to change it. But the reality is that I need not have had so little confidence in my abilities. Measurable intelligence is largely a product of application – if we apply effective methods of learning in the right way, then we are all as able as each other to store and retrieve data. Memory training enables us to strengthen our ability to learn – we know that training our memory can raise our IQ. So, the skills of concentration, imagination and association – all of which are key memory skills – make us brighter too.

Theories of Forgetting

How long does memory last? What factors govern forgetting? The so-called "trace-decay theory" claims that the neural connections that form particular memories (see p.42) may fade and, if they are not used regularly, disappear. Currently, this is impossible to prove. A more popular view is that, once something is committed to long-term memory, it is never lost, and only requires the appropriate association to bring it to mind. Over the course of a lifetime, however, a number of different memories may come to share many of the same cues. In this case it will be difficult to select out any one memory in particular, unless there are exceptional reasons (additional cues) for doing so. For example, we can probably remember our first day at school, as well as the worst day. But most of our school days are too insignificant to have specific cues that differentiate one day from another. They have not been lost from memory, but they have been buried in a shapeless cluster within our mind. Nevertheless, in principle there will be cues, however subtle, that will allow us to recover every single day if we work at doing so.

Memory is a net; one finds it full of fish when he takes it from the brook; but a dozen miles of water have run through it without sticking.

Oliver Wendell Holmes, Sr 1858

According to this theory, memories become hard to find because they "take over" each other's cues. Interference is both *proactive inhibition* (an existing memory inhibits the new one because the cues are monopolized by the older memory) and *retroactive inhibition* (a new memory blocks our ability to recall old information because the new memory "steals" the older memory's cues). Someone memorizing two different lists of city names on consecutive days will recall either list less accurately than someone with a list of city names and a list of dog breeds.

Proactive inhibition works partly because it causes us to make approximations. If we see a breed of dog that we cannot identify but which resembles a corgi, we will store it as "something that is quite like a corgi but not one". If asked to recall the appearance of the dog, our memories will bring to mind a corgi and we are likely to have forgotten precisely the distinctive features of the actual breed we need to recall. But retroactive inhibition appears to be the more persistent mechanism in forgetting, because it seems to cause old memories to be "unlearned" and is easily suggestible by logic. When we learn new aspects of a topic, drawing different conclusions from the ones already learned, the new aspects will cause the older theories to be hard to fathom, because the memory of their logic is lost.

Déjà Vu

Déjà vu ("already seen") is the often disconcerting feeling of re-experiencing something – of treading on ground we seem to have trodden before. For example, we may be engaged in a conversation and feel that we have had exactly the same interaction on a previous occasion. One theory about *déjà vu* is that when the features of a current experience are similar to a previous one, the details of which seem forgotten, the mind fills in the blanks, creating a real but misleading memory from a few fragments. Another explanation is that an event may be transferred by the unconscious straight into long-term memory and then reactivated from there. Of course, we may simply have forgotten a previous, similar experience, making our apparent recognition of the current event baffling.

Lost Memory

In extreme circumstances a memory can be so unbearable that the person who has had the experience will prefer temporarily to deny – or to wipe out – their entire personal histories rather than face that one memory. Sufferers of *psychogenic amnesia* (also known as "hysterical" or "fugue" amnesia) may be able to recite the alphabet or remember how to work complex machinery, but will be unable to give their names, addresses or any personal details. The psychogenic amnesiac usually recovers after a few days, and there seems to be no structural damage to the brain. Some researchers believe that the victim's memories have been disconnected from one another; others do not actually believe in the condition, claiming that it represents a conscious refusal to remember, rather than a genuine inability.

The most common cause of amnesia is a blow to the head. When a football player is knocked unconscious, he first suffers *post-traumatic amnesia* – defined as a period of unconsciousness accompanied by a resulting confusion and an inability to say exactly where he is. When this phase is over, he may have *retrograde amnesia* – the inability to remember events before the accident, sometimes stretching back as far as several years. As he recovers, the earlier memories come back first, and his blank spell retreats to a point several minutes before the accident. But those last few minutes are almost without exception never recovered, because the trauma has interfered with their consolidation. For a time during recovery, the football player may also suffer from *anterograde amnesia*, or a difficulty in learning new facts. This seems to be a problem with consolidating long-term memory, because tests reveal the short-term memory to be unaffected by anterograde amnesia.

Another type of amnesia occurs if we suffer damage to the hippocampus and thalamus (through such conditions as encephalitis, stroke, a prolonged period of drinking too much, or vitamin B_1 deficiency). People with this problem often have good recall of the past and normal short-term memories, but they are unable to recall what they had for breakfast only an hour ago. Their procedural memory (see p.38) seems unaffected. If allowed to play with the same puzzle, day after day, their procedural memory will enable them to become steadily faster at solving it, even though they never remember having solved it before.

The Power of Suggestion

Hypnosis (a deep state of relaxation, akin to sleeping) usually brought about by external suggestion. Psychoanalysts use it to help patients recall blocked memories. A person in a hypnotic state is able to respond to instructions and answer questions.

Responses to hypnosis vary considerably from one individual to the next, as does the clarity of the memories that are recalled. Some people have been able to recall their experience of their mother's womb and of birth. Why hypnosis works is not altogether clear, but it is thought that during deep relaxation we are able to make more fluid associations in our minds (just as we do when we dream), which permits us to find more cues to take us to certain apparently forgotten memories.

Memory in Children

How old are babies before they begin to remember? And can a fetus learn in the womb? In early infancy we lack a consciousness of ourselves as individuals. As a result, experts used to think that we could not possibly have memories, because we could not recognize events as happening to us. In fact, at the moment of birth, infants already have a preference for their mother's voice, presumably because its characteristic timbre has already been learned *in utero*. The neurons in the brain of the human fetus experience a growth spurt that starts some ten weeks before birth. New axons begin to proliferate, increasing the opportunity for communication between the dendrites and axons of other neurons. This process allows the formation of memory (see pp.40–43).

Most researchers now agree with the instincts of many mothers that their babies recognize them within only a few of days of birth. It seems that memory – however rudimentary – precedes consciousness, and not the other way round. It can be argued that memories – and a sense of continuity between them – are the necessary building blocks for any permanent sense of self.

At around eight or nine months, infants begin to show clear signs of having developed explicit and short-term memory (see pp.36–7). They begin to gesture to specific objects that they want, and can search for objects after they have been hidden. Several months to a year later, the child is already acquiring language, and therefore developing semantic memory (see pp.37–8). However, a child's semantic memory is much more fluid than an adult's, and grows by a combination of loose association and trial and error. In one case, a child first used the word "quah" for a duck on a pond, then for a liquid, then a coin with an eagle on it, then any coin-like round object. Similarly, a child who learns the word "ball" may then use it for a balloon, anything that can be bounced, a rounded pebble, and so on.

The child's mind appears to be constantly experimenting, testing, adopting and rejecting new hypotheses about the external world. As a result, its memories are not as stable as they will become in adulthood. This also explains why the child's grasp of facts will appear to progress in fits and starts, and why language skills that seem to have been securely learned can temporarily seem to disappear.

A Perfect Picture

Eidetic (photographic) memory is when we can recall something perfectly after only a brief glance. We marvel at such a feat in adults, but many children display this ability naturally. In the early nineteenth century, the tests of G.W. Allport in England and E.R. Jaensch in Germany found that children aged between 10 and 13 could answer detailed questions about pictures they had looked at for only 35 seconds, including, for example, the number of stripes in a picture of a zebra. There have been surprisingly few studies of eidetic memory since that time, but it is suggested that between eight and 50 per cent of children under the age of 11 possess this eidetic ability. Psychologists think that its loss (usually during adolescence) may be due to the emphasis placed on verbal skills during education.

Memory and Aging

The claim that our memory will let us down when we get old is a myth. It is not at all inevitable that we will suffer memory loss as we approach our twilight years. However, what is inevitable is that the speed at which our brain processes and stores our memories will change. This is the principal reason why older people tend to do less well on timed IQ tests than younger candidates. But, if older people are given more time to complete the exercises, the average results tend to be the same as those for the youngsters.

Part of the reason why the brain's processes slow down as we age begins with the slowing down of our circulation. In old age, a lifetime of wear and tear takes its toll on our heart and arteries, so that it takes longer for oxygenated blood to reach the brain in the quantities needed for peak performance (the brain is the single most oxygen-consuming organ in the body). The neurons are highly sensitive to reductions in oxygen supply, which cause them to have less energy. If the neurons have less energy, the levels to which the dendrites become excited when we consolidate or retrieve memories are reduced.

Under normal, healthy circumstances, the ability to recall our long-term memories does not change throughout our lives (although our short-term memory may show some depreciation). This is because the levels of RNA (which controls the manufacture of proteins in brain cells, resulting in larger synapses and better consolidation of memories) increases in our brain as we age.

In fact, many scientists now believe that social stereotyping is one of the factors that may contribute to forgetfulness in older people. Because we expect that our memory will deteriorate as we get older, we unconsciously place greater significance on the items or occasions that we actually do forget in daily life (while in youthfulness we used to simply let such instances of forgetfulness wash over us). This in turn makes us anxious that we are becoming old and less mentally agile. Of course, anxiety really does impair our powers of memory, so as soon as we become worried about aging and loss of memory we may indeed become the archetypal "forgetful grandparent", in a self-fulfilling prophecy.

So, whatever else you remember, be sure to remember this – having confidence in the indestructibility of your memory is, more often than not, half the battle to a permanently brilliant ability to remember. And that is true whether we are 10 or 110 years old!

Use It or Lose It

Our brains are more likely to remain alert throughout our lives if we keep them healthy. Just as we take exercise to keep our bodies physically fit, and watch our diet to avoid illness, so we need to take care of our brain. Memory training provides an excellent mental workout, and if we make memory exercises part of our daily lives, and continue to expect our memory to serve us well, it is more likely to remain up to the task. Research carried out in Japan showed that a group of people aged over 80 had greater mental agility and memory power than contemporaries who were in their sixties. The difference was that the octogenarians had continued working. We don't have to stay in employment, but finding daily mental stimulation will help to keep our memory in good condition, whatever our age.

CHAPTER THREE

ENTICING THE ECHOES

How to improve your memory

The first step in improving our memories is to have faith in memory as a perfectible faculty. We may speak of having a memory "like a sieve" – yet this is not the same order of reality as being balding, or colour-blind, or pigeon-toed. As you begin to use simple memory techniques, you will find that your ability to recall facts, events, places and people gradually sharpens. Memory depends on three basic processes: making something memorable, storing that item in the mind, and recalling it accurately at some future time.

In this chapter, we look at the ways in which the basic operation of our memory may be improved by applying the arts of imagination, association, location, concentration and observation. We also discover how physical health enhances memory and how our senses help us to hold information. Lastly we look at some of the principles of memory recall.

The Memory Gymnasium

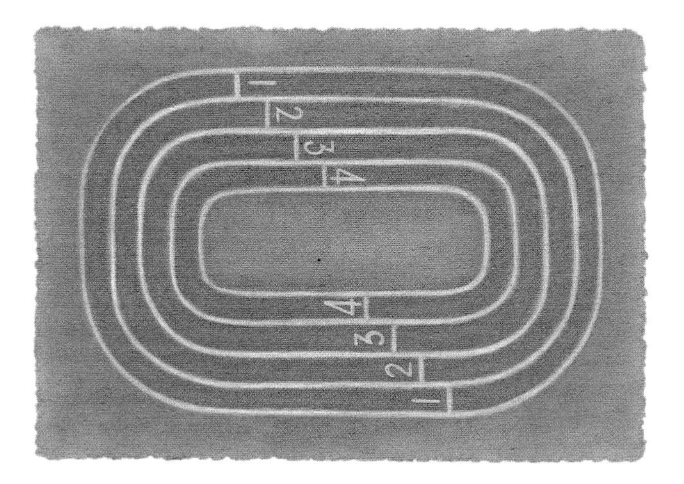

Visualize for a minute 10 billion neurons in your brain. Think how, as you read the words on the page, electrical impulses streak through your cerebrum, making the millions of connections necessary for you to understand the meaning of this text. Now imagine how wonderful it would be if each one of those connections could be stronger. Doing just that is what memory training is all about – tapping into latent brain power to make our minds faster, brighter and altogether more powerful.

Apart from learning how to memorize and recall information properly, there are many other benefits to be gleaned from memory training. The constant stimulation of the mind improves all our mental faculties, from our ability to concentrate on a novel or rationalize an argument to our aptitude for appreciating a work of art. As we memorize we make new neural connections in our brains so that the transfer of chemicals between neurons takes place faster and more easily. In this way, when we come to access information, our brains can work more efficiently.

The brain is not a muscle, but for the purpose of demonstrating the changes that memory training can bring about, muscles provide a good analogy. The more we use our mind, the "stronger" it appears to grow. We all know what it feels like to have all our mental faculties concentrated on a particular situation – time passes quickly, we take pleasure in the resolution that our own mental efforts are bringing about, we have a sense of being fully engaged, and of being mentally "fitter". But whereas muscles have a threshold of potential, our memory has limitless power – we are physically unable to use up all the space that lies available within it. However, if we do not stimulate our brains by giving them enough work to do, like an unused muscle our mental capacity grows weaker and certain mental tasks that once seemed easy now seem beyond our grasp. Try testing this by spending a week doing a simple puzzle every day – say, the quick crossword in your daily newspaper. As the week progresses, the puzzles should become quicker to solve. Then, stop doing the puzzles for a week or so. When you begin again, do they seem more difficult than they were just before you stopped?

The changes that occur are not just in the realm of mental agility. Research has shown that the more we use our brains in this way, the denser and larger they actually become.

Spend fifteen minutes a day sharpening your ability to remember simple events. Last thing at night, try to remember the order of the things that you did during the day. Zoom in on specific conversations, your surroundings and even what you were thinking or feeling in each of the day's situations. With practice, as you begin to recapture and concentrate upon the events of the day, the details should more readily flood back to you.

The Art of Memory

If your mind were a room, what would it look like? For most of us, it would be true to say that the mind resembles an attic, with well-organized and accessible items close to the doorway, but with all sorts of treasures (including family heirlooms and bric-a-brac) randomly piled out of reach in the shadows further back. To look for something that has lain unused for a year or two might take us some time – and we could never be sure of finding it. However, perhaps it's time for a clear-out? If we can learn to make better use of the storage space available, we might be able to retain and recall information more effectively.

A far-fetched comparison, you might think, and one that is bound to oversimplify the complexities of the mind – which after all is one of the wonders of human biology. Yet in fact, for practical purposes, this analogy is perfectly accurate. If we want to understand how memory operates, we can think of ourselves as filing a piece of information, literally, in an appropriate compartment in the filing system. The art of storing, retaining and recalling memories is really a matter of getting organized – sorting out our mental clutter, so to speak – so that the next time we need to access a certain piece of information, it is logically placed for us to find.

Oblivion is the dark page, whereon Memory writes her light-beam characters, and makes them legible.

Thomas Carlyle
1833

We have seen how the brain is divided into two hemispheres – the left brain, which processes logic and language; and the right brain, which processes the creative side of ourselves. Memory, in so far as it requires logical organization, is in large measure a left-brain activity – in this respect you might think of memory as an applied science. But memory is also an art, because the information we

receive through our senses can be made memorable through creative use of our imagination. This combination of logical and creative thought links the networks of the entire brain together, like bridges over a river, making our minds more efficient at creating, storing and retrieving every kind of memory.

The main techniques offered in this book for training and enhancing your memory bear similarities to approaches used by the ancient Greeks (see pp.16–17). During ten years of studying memory, and training my own mind, I have boiled down the methods of the ancients to three main ingredients: imagination (transforming new information into images that we can retain in our mind); association (connecting these imaginative images to what we already know); and location (anchoring these associations in our mind in the manner of the old Greek method of *loci*, or "places"). The basic principles behind all these elements are given on pp.68–75. Here and there in this book I also offer further methods, ranging from simple mnemonics (usually word-based) to the visual-peg system, which may be regarded as a halfway stage to the locus method. The latter reaches its most elaborate development in the journey method, which I favour for the most demanding tasks of memorization – including World Memory Championships.

Location is especially helpful when a sequence of data has to be committed to memory in a particular order. Combined with the other two key ingredients – imagination and association – we have the power to remember any number of facts we wish. Before going on to describe the principles behind each of the three elements in more detail, it may be useful, by way of a "taster", to give an example of imagination and association in use.

Essentially, the most basic skill of the art of memory is to create a mental symbol for each piece of information we wish to retain. Let us say that you want to remember the following facts connected with historic expeditions to the South Pole. Roald Amundsen travelled to the Pole on skis; Ernest Shackleton travelled with dogs; Robert Falcon Scott travelled, foolishly, with ponies. First, you need to visualize these events in mental snapshots. This is the process of engagement – that is, turning the words into a meaning that you fully engage with in your mind. Then you need to find a visual association that links the mode of transport to the names that you already (perhaps vaguely) know. Roald might suggest "rolled" – so you imagine Amundsen rolling over on his skis. Shackleton makes you think of the dogs "shackled" to their sledges (you might additionally think of them "earnestly" moving across the icefields); Falcon suggests the bird, hovering above the real world – as Scott was when he chose such an unsuitable method of transport for Antarctic conditions. Memorizing the information this way helps you to fix in your mind not only the means of travel but also the first names of these famous explorers (actually, in Scott's case, the middle name, but once that is committed to memory you will probably find the first name easier to recall).

Once we have our images filed away in our minds, we need to make sure that they can be retained for as long as we need them – perhaps a few days, perhaps indefinitely. One of the most effective methods is to repeat what we have stored – with each revision the impression on our memory becomes deeper (see pp.80–81).

Charting Your Progress

The memory techniques in this book are best used as part of a conscious program of memory training. You might try using the visual-peg system or the journey method to memorize random data, monitoring your progress (testing yourself) as you go. In the early stages of memory improvement, this is likely to be hard work. Giving yourself quantifiable goals for your memory training helps you to track the progress of your powers of retention and, more importantly, helps you to retain your enthusiasm. Many of the exercises in this book provide self-tests, but don't do them just once – modify them, keep practising them. You will see improvements beginning to show in your records sooner than you may think. And the increased motivation this brings will almost certainly spur you on to even greater success.

The Art of Imagination

According to the ancient Greek philosopher Aristotle (384–322BCE), imagination and memory are inexorably linked, because they belong to the same part of the soul. Whether or not we believe in the soul's existence, it is natural for us to accept that imagination and memory go hand in hand. Like memory, imagination uses both sides of the brain. We employ our imagination as a kind of symbolic converter, transforming the linear, systematic information that is processed by our left brain into vivid, creative information to which our right brain responds.

At a practical level, it is important for us to recognize that imagination is a key factor in the regular operation of memory, and an aspect on which we need to concentrate if we are trying to make our memory more efficient. Advanced memory techniques, as we shall see, require us to stretch our imagination to lengths that the rational, logical part of the brain might initially find somewhat alien.

Look back over experiences that you criticized at the time as forgettable – perhaps a biography that did not hold your concentration or a radio talk during which you fell asleep. When we complain that something is forgettable, often what we are really saying is that the experience was unexciting – it failed to fire our imagination. Looked at another way, if something is to be memorable, it helps for it to be imaginative.

Effective use of memory requires us to enliven even potentially mundane pieces of information – a set of numbers, a shopping list, a sequence of street directions. The first step in achieving this transformation is mental imaging – we literally picture the

real thing (the number 56, a carton of cranberry juice, a left turn by the city clock) in our mind. Then we take the realistic mental image and, using visualization, we turn it into something that is experienced in a number of different aspects. While holding in our mind a clear picture of how the thing looks, we might imagine at the same time how it stimulates the other senses. Does it have a smell? Can we taste it? What does it feel like to touch? How does it sound? However, even conjuring up a sensual experience is not usually enough to make the item memorable, so we need to give it a new dimension – we need to use our imagination. This means stepping into a world of infinite possibilities, where exciting and memorable impressions are soon brought into being. So if, for example, we want to remember to buy oranges, we might visualize them blazing in the sky like miniature suns. Or if a can of tuna is on our shopping list, we might imagine the can with fins, swimming in a shoal with its fellow fishes.

Conferring movement and life on inanimate objects, or making humans or animals behave or change shape in unlikely ways, will help to fix an impression in your mind. The more surreal the image, the more retrievable it is likely to be. The purpose of such image-making is to embellish the item that you want to store, in order to invest it with enhanced interior presence. We may not immediately remember the item, but in theory we will remember the scenario that we have created for it – or even the act of creating the scenario.

We all know that imagination is the quality that distinguishes the creative artist, and reflecting on this might make us feel a little awkward at first in aspiring to be imaginative ourselves. Yet in fact our imagination comes into play every time we look forward to an expedition, an evening out or a vacation (we imagine what it will be like), or conjure up a visual image as a friend relates an amusing story. In our own inner theatre of the mind, nothing lies beyond our capability. How will I be able to come up with such odd and unexpected transformations, you might ask yourself? All it takes is confidence – underpinned by faith in the imagination as a main thoroughfare toward an enhanced memory. Experiment – you may be surprised how quickly this way of thinking becomes second nature.

Like our memory, our imagination becomes more agile with use. It becomes increasingly easy to weave aspects of daily life into vivid and surreal transformations. As we observe this development in ourselves, we should take heart – imaginative invention of this kind is the key to many of the specific memory techniques described in the next chapter.

Painting a Memory Masterpiece

EXERCISE FOUR

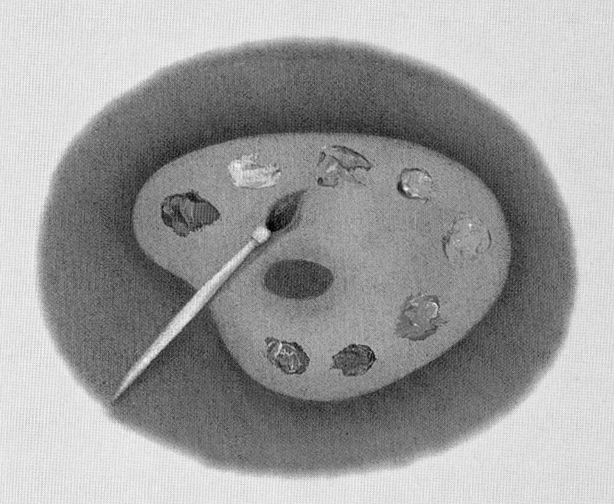

Imagination enables us to conjure surreal and memorable imagery. In this exercise, we practise this aspect of memorization by "painting" a vivid mental picture of an item on a shopping list. The process involves "morphing" the item – changing its appearance in the mind's eye, in order to fix a firmer impression that we will more readily be able to recall.

1. Imagine an apple in as much detail as you can. Is it red or green? Is it large or small? Is it perfect or bruised? Is it ripe or unripe? As you make these decisions, imagine a picture evolving that shows the apple in realistic detail.

2. Contemplate your mental picture in its finished form. Can you change the apple to make it more remarkable? You might imagine it giant-sized. If it were as big as a basketball, would you bounce it or roll it home? If it had human features, who would these belong to? Perhaps the healthiest-looking of your friends, or someone with rosy cheeks?

3. Take another item from your shopping list, such as an egg, and exaggerate or embellish it in a similar way. Do this with five different items. Next time you actually go to the store, see if you can remember a "virtual shopping" list, using such images as triggers. Then, next time, lengthen the list to 10 items. Experiment with variations on this exercise.

The Art of Association

An association is a mental link between two disparate items. We make associations all the time. Take, for example, a hypothetical situation in which you are walking back to work at lunchtime when you see a mail van pass by. The van sparks off the memory that earlier in the day you resolved to mail something. In turn, you recall that what you have to mail is your mother's birthday card. The connections that you make in your head from one thought to another happen in a split second, and you would not normally pause to notice the links; yet they are an important part of recollection. When I began to train my memory, I soon realized that the associations I had made throughout my life were reconnecting, enabling me to recall not only what I had purposely memorized but also previously forgotten life experiences.

Many associations occur naturally and spontaneously, as a result of inherent meaning or cultural tradition. For example, a golf club is associated by function with a fishing rod, because both are implements used in a leisure activity. Spectacles are associated with scholarship or intelligence, through a perceived link with reading. Successful memory work involves using natural associations of this kind as well as forging new, unnatural associations to link a forgettable item of information with an unforgettable image.

For example, on meeting someone at a party you are told that his name is Horace Washington. These names may be easier to remember if you think of natural associations – Horace, the Roman poet; Washington, DC, the city. You now have concrete mental associations that are more interesting and meaningful than merely the sound or spelling of the names. If the person you have just met strikes you as being something of a dreamer, then you might link this characteristic with the idea of a poet as a weaver of dreams – and this will perhaps drive the name even more deeply into your memory. If the person seems rather untidy in thought, manner or appearance, you might contrast this with the symmetrical city plan of Washington, DC. You now have mental associations that relate to the two names *and* to the person. This reinforcing effect makes it even less likely that you will forget the names in the future.

Now it might be objected that this example is artificial: it depends on the person being a dreamer, whereas in fact this would be a highly unlikely coincidence. But there will always be some association that can be made to work, however indirectly. Say, for example, that the person has a reputation for unpunctuality. The name Horace might then trigger an ironic sound association with Oris, a Swiss watch manufacturer. Or alternatively, the person might seem slow in speech, prompting you to break Horace down punningly into two words – "Ho!", expressing surprise; "race", suggesting speed.

All these associative techniques, based on the sense and sound of words, can play a part in the storage (and so, by extension, the retrieval) of memories.

The Art of Location

We saw earlier (pp.17–18) that the Greeks and Romans valued the art of location above all others in relation to memory. The locus method was their fundamental principle of memorization. I believe that this time-honoured principle is, without doubt, the key to my success at six World Memory Championships. Placing each piece of data that I had to absorb in a particular place that I had already set aside in my mind made it easier for me to recall those items. And through practice I became proficient.

Just as we use association all the time without noticing that we are doing so, the same is true of location. Think about the events that happened to you over the course of the day. What did you do? If you were to describe your day in detail to a friend, the chances are that location would figure prominently in your recollections: "I got up and went to the kitchen to put on some coffee, then I went to the bathroom and had a shower, before sitting in the kitchen and eating my breakfast ... " and so on. Studies show that people who have spent the day travelling are especially accurate in recalling the sequence of events in the day. Even details of conversations seem sharper because the dialogue is remembered in the setting in which it took place. The various locations in which we find ourselves while travelling serve as a linear mental framework that throws into sharp relief our particular experiences.

Further evidence for the importance of location in the art of memory is found in the common problem of losing our keys. We all know how frustrating it is to be rushing in the morning to leave for an appointment only to find that we cannot remember where we put the keys to the front door. What most of us do (perfectly logically) to trigger the memory is retrace our steps. The last time we came into the house we must have had the keys in our hand, and we then went straight to the study to check our telephone messages. But the keys are not there, so we continue to retrace our steps (literally or figuratively) into the hallway, where we went to hang up our coat. And so we continue, until eventually we arrive at the place where we had put down the keys and, usually, we find them again. We do all this using the art of location.

Locus-based memory systems work because the location is fixed, so that we can always walk ourselves mentally back through the same places to pick up the various pieces of information that we deposited there. This system of anchoring is an important point about location. When we use the art of location, we position images or data (or anything else that we want to remember, such as key points in a speech) in a tangible, fixed place in our mind, such as the image of a house that we know well or a familiar journey. When we want to remember the information, we retrace our steps and find that the data is still moored there, where we left it. We will soon go on to discover specific techniques for choosing the most effective mental locations and anchoring the data most reliably.

The journey method (pp.102–7) takes the location principle to its furthest and most impressive extreme, enabling us to memorize and recall surprisingly large quantities of data (for example, I use it to remember simultaneously the order of randomly shuffled cards in multiple decks). Location may be an ancient technique, but it is certainly one of the most powerful memory aids.

The Art of Concentration

One of the biggest enemies to perfect recall occurs within the first few seconds of our attempts to memorize. The problem lies not with our having an innately bad memory (we all have a good memory, most of us have merely forgotten how to use its full potential), but with our levels of concentration. To concentrate is to notice what we see, to listen to what we hear, to feel what we touch, to savour what we taste and smell, and to be mindful of what we think. The secret of concentration when formally memorizing is to focus fully on the information that we are being told or the experience that we are having, while at the same time allowing our brain to make appropriate associations – for example, the mental picture of the places that we have preselected according to the locus principle. During this process the data passes from our short-term to our long-term memory, where it is stored ready for us to recall as and when we want it.

Just as eating against one's will is injurious to health, so study without a liking for it spoils the memory, and it retains nothing it takes in.

Leonardo da Vinci
c.1500

The crucial thing here is the ability to focus. We might think that we are able to concentrate on more than one thing at once – say, reading a book and watching a news item on television. However, scientifically, such split focus is impossible. If we try to do two things at once, our attention flits back and forth at lightning speed between the two, and we concentrate fully on neither. When you attempt a purposeful memorization, it is important to focus on the items and the system by which you remember them, without allowing external stimuli to influence your concentration at all. The mind is capable of 100 per cent concentration. I practise meditation to train my mind to become fully attentive. When I go to memorize, I spend a few moments recapturing the focus that the practice gives.

A Memory Meditation Warm-up

EXERCISE FIVE

When you use memorization techniques such as those described in the next chapter, you will need to be able to slow your brain waves to a state of full concentration. Practise by following this meditation exercise.

1. Choose a quiet room for your meditation, where you will be undisturbed. Place a cushion on the floor to support your neck and lie down on your back. Keep your arms loosely at your sides, palms up. Let your feet flop outward naturally.

2. Close your eyes. Breathe in slowly and deeply through your nostrils. As you breathe in, your diaphragm should expand, raising your abdomen then your chest. Exhale slowly through your mouth. Continue breathing in this manner throughout the meditation.

3. Focus your attention on the imaginary space just behind your eyes. Imagine that a small, bright light is floating there. Channel all your attention into the light.

4. Imagine that the white light is expanding and shrinking with your in- and out-breaths. In your mind's eye, watch it glow brighter as you breathe in and dim as you breathe out. Stay focused like this for as long as you feel comfortable. Try to practise a meditation such as this at least once a day, to encourage your powers of concentration.

The Art of Observation

The ancient Greeks considered sight to be the most important of the senses in relation to memory. They believed that the sharper our powers of observation, the more accurate our memory of experiences. There is truth in this, although actually the overall picture is more complex – we memorize better if we use all our senses fully.

Nevertheless, the Greeks had a point. When we observe an object in a fully attentive, fully conscious way (noting colour, shape, size, distinguishing features), the etchings that are made on the brain are deeper than when we merely receive an overall visual impression. Mostly, we just glance, or stare using only part of our attention. For example, think of a bird with distinctive markings, one that you regularly see. Draw a sketch of the bird showing where the patches of colour occur. Check your drawing the next time you see the real thing: you may be surprised at the mistakes you have made.

If you pay attention, the judgment will better perceive the things going through the mind.

Dialexeis
400BCE

At a mundane level, honing our powers of observation has particular benefits for our ability to recall, say, street directions on a repeated journey. When describing the route to a stranger who has asked the way, it obviously helps to be able to visualize the various landmarks. But in a more subtle sense, being able to recall precise visual details in the mind's eye is part of a discipline of mental focus and alertness that is sure to feed back beneficially into our memory training. Concentrating on the details of how things look will inevitably make them more interesting and therefore more memorable. This in turn is likely to help our powers of association – which, as we have seen, are a vital tool in the process of committing something permanently to memory.

Noticing the Details

EXERCISE SIX

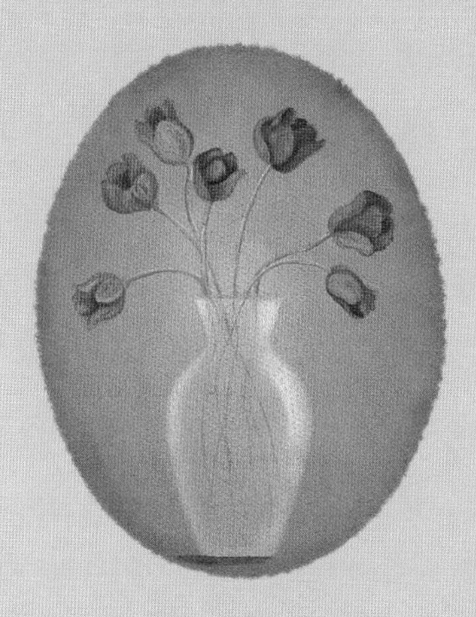

Honing your powers of observation is highly beneficial for memorization and recall. Use this exercise to reduce the "perceptual filtering" that occurs when you look at something, so that what is there is truly what you see.

1. Take a pencil and piece of paper, and choose a vase of flowers or some other object to draw. Your level of artistic ability is completely unimportant – the sole purpose is to learn to observe a scene and recreate that scene in the mind's eye in as much detail as possible.

2. Spend five minutes or so noticing as many features of the vase and flowers as you can. Does the vase have a pattern? How many petals do the flowers have? Are the flowers fully open? What are the veins in the leaves like? Don't fall into the trap of missing the obvious things (colour, shape, number, and so on) in looking for the details.

3. Look away and draw the vase. Annotate your picture to indicate colours and any details you cannot fully capture by drawing. Look back at the vase and compare it with your annotated sketch. How accurate were your observations of colour, shape and proportion? What did you miss? Repeat the exercise regularly with a range of different objects to hone your powers of observation.

Revision and Repetition

Learning by rote – the repetition of facts over and over until they become firmly lodged in the mind – has been largely discredited in education. This is partly because the rote method is purely mechanical – whereas we now believe that the most memorable facts are those that engage our interest, that involve us in some way. However, there is no doubt that repetition, in one of its senses, has a vital part to play in memory work. This is not a matter of chanting information like a class of Victorian schoolchildren, so that we recall the sound before we recall the sense. Rather, it is a matter of rehearsing an act of memory, going over the process of recall, at regular intervals, to fix the various routes of association in your mind.

It is difficult to give precise guidelines on how often, and how soon after the memorization, recall should be practised in this way. Much depends on the type of information involved, and the method by which you memorize it. Obviously, if you commit a phone number to memory, with a view to dialling that number in ten minutes' time, your rehearsals need to be squeezed into that particular time frame. Repetition would in this case be valuable, indeed essential, even if you were to use no memory system at all – in other words, if you were to follow the rote method. However, if someone interrupted you during your repetition exercise, there would be a strong possibility of your forgetting the number altogether. So a better approach would be to use some variation of the DOMINIC system (see pp.108–9) or the number-shape system (see pp.110–11), and rehearse not the number itself, but your encoded version of the number – and the retranslation of that code back into the number.

If you are faced with the challenge of absorbing information in a magazine article, on the other hand, you might consider following the "rule of five", whereby you repeat the key points to yourself after one hour, then a day later, then a week later, then two weeks later, then a month later. This would be valid whatever memory system you used for fixing the facts in the first place. However, you would probably benefit from a handful of rehearsals in the first five minutes after encoding the data, before applying the rule of five.

Every time we recall a piece of information, the route to it becomes strengthened, in the way that a path becomes clearer and easier to walk along if it is well trodden. Repetition does not guarantee recall, but certainly rewards the time spent with a greater chance of accurate memorization.

Memory and Health

Over the centuries people have looked for physical ways to tune their memories. In the seventeenth century it was believed by some North Americans that wearing a beaverskin cap would enhance their recall. At other times the favoured treatment has been a few drops of castor oil rubbed into the head or the back.

While health fads will always come and go, we now realize that one of the most effective ways to improve our recall and keep our memory in optimum working order is to keep fit. A well-nourished body is one of the keys to a well-nourished mind.

Most experts agree that the path to fitness is simple: take regular exercise and eat a healthy diet. Whether your exercise is 20 lengths of the swimming pool every other day or a daily brisk walk around the block, if it gets your limbs moving and your heart beating faster it increases the blood flow to your brain. This blood feeds our neurons with oxygen and nutrients, keeping them healthy. My own practice is to run every morning (or at least as often as I can) and play golf regularly; when I'm in training for a memory competition, I gradually step up the length of the runs. However, the exertion need not be strenuous for your brain to feel the benefit.

Evidence suggests that the leaves of the *Ginkgo biloba* tree (in ancient times this was known as the "tree of memory") can help to improve memory by increasing blood flow to the brain. The German philosopher Johann Wolfgang von Goethe (1749–1832), who retained his mental agility well into old age, was said to eat a ginkgo leaf with his breakfast every morning.

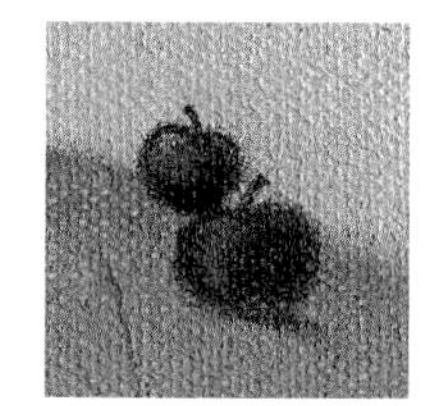

Studies have shown that if we maintain a low-calorie diet, even for a short period, our memory performance is noticeably poorer than when we eat foods with a full complement of nutrients. The calories in food give us energy, which our body uses to power our brains (as well as our other organs). If our brain is starved of energy, then our memory is one of the first functions to falter.

Foods that are rich in the antioxidant vitamins A, C and (more especially) E are particularly beneficial to the health of the brain and therefore that of the memory. These vitamins are found in richly coloured fruit and vegetables, such as bananas, red peppers, spinach and oranges, among others. They help to "mop up" chemicals known as free radicals, which are naturally present in the body, but which, when we overproduce them (usually if we are under stress or subject to the harmful effects of pollution), can cause extensive cell damage in the brain (as well as in other parts of the body).

Your prayer must be for a sound mind in a sound body.

Juvenal
*c.*60–*c.*130CE

Another good tip is to eat plenty of oily fish. This is so important for the health of our minds that it is often nicknamed "brain food". Oily fish contains folic acid and several essential fatty acids – all of which are vital in the development and functioning of the brain and nervous system. Try to include fish in your diet at least twice a week. Other sources of protein (such as white meat, dairy products and tofu) have similar, if not so pronounced, benefits for memory.

Memory and the Senses

Incorporating all our five senses into whatever memory techniques we favour will make it easier for us to memorize and recall. Let us say that one of the techniques we use involves imagining a tree. When we conjure up that tree in our minds, the more realistic our image, the more realized the memory. At the simplest level, we might conjure up merely a two-dimensional image of a tree. But if instead we imagine an oak, in full leaf, with a light wind whistling through its leaves, and the smells of summer all around, this will make a deeper impression. It will also give us more potential associations to make with any item we wish to store alongside the tree.

I had recognized the taste of the crumb of madeleine soaked in her concoction of lime-flowers which my aunt used to give me ... immediately the old grey house upon the street, where her room was, rose up like the scenery of a theatre.

Marcel Proust
1871–1922

As a general rule, the most powerful senses for recall are sight, sound and smell. Sight is the basic interpretative sense, which we crucially use for navigation. Sound is the main method by which we communicate with others. Both sight and sound play a part in memorizing words and numbers, which otherwise can have an elusive abstract quality. Smell and taste are particularly powerful memory cues, possibly because these senses were once so important to our survival. Smell bypasses the thalamus region of the brain stem, and connects directly with the neurons in the cortex – creating a direct route to our memory store. This is why a scent can instantly transport us back to a highly emotive event in our past, or remind us so strongly of a particular person. Spend some time trying to recognize the smells that have particular significance for you. Think of this as part of a sensory tuning designed to open up your mind more fully to your experiences – the beneficial effects for your memory training will follow on naturally.

The Memory Kaleidoscope

EXERCISE SEVEN

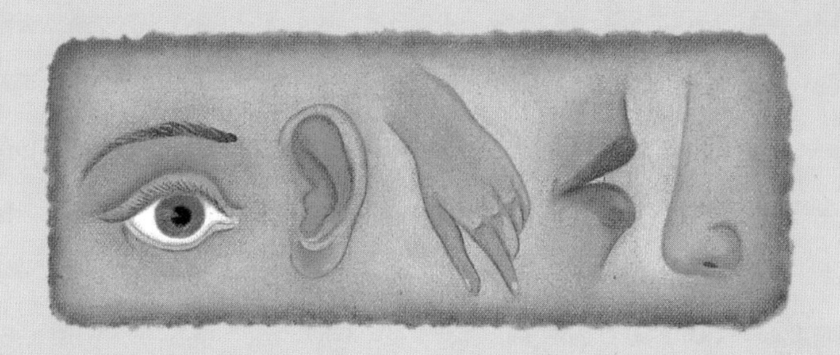

All too often we rely solely upon sight when conjuring something up in our minds. This visualization exercise is intended to help you appreciate the significance of the other senses. At the same time it stretches the imagination in ways that benefit the practice of memory techniques.

1. Close your eyes and imagine a complex yet readily identifiable item, such as a racehorse and jockey. Visualize the horse and its rider meticulously in your imagination – the colourful blouson of the rider, the harness and saddle, the fine, proud expression on the horse's face, the jockey's face shadowed under the peak of his cap.

2. In turn, think of aspects of touch, sound, smell and taste associated with the image. For touch, you might think of the satiny texture of the jockey's blouson, the smoothly groomed coat of the horse, the coarse hair of the mane; for sound, the galloping hooves and the cheering crowd; for smell, the leather and the sweat; for taste, perhaps a sugar lump fed to the horse before the race (feel at the same time the horse's slurpy tongue on your fingers).

3. This is just one random example. Now think of other readily identifiable images to treat in the same way. It does not matter if one or two of the senses at first seem irrelevant to the image – you will eventually think of ways of bringing them in, even if you have to resort to surreal imaginings.

Memory and Music

Many people prefer to read or study in silence, while others favour some kind of background music. Although we might think of music (especially rhythmic rock) as hostile to concentration, it has been shown that in certain circumstances music can create an atmosphere that encourages mental absorption. In the 1960s the Bulgarian psychologist Georgi Lozanov found in an experiment that when slow Baroque music was played, some people showed greatly improved learning compared with others who had learned in silence or to the accompaniment of other musical genres. This and further scientific investigations have shown that the ideal music for learning (and so for optimum recall) has a slow, relaxing tempo of one beat per second.

Music, when soft voices die, Vibrates in the memory.

Percy Shelley
1821

You could test this yourself: try memorizing a random list of 15 numbers while listening to a slow movement by, say, the composers Handel, Bach or Vivaldi. Then try to memorize another list of 15 numbers in silence, and compare your success in both trials. The experiment is crude (there are many other factors at work to influence how much you can recall accurately), but you may be pleasantly surprised to find that music appears to help your ability to remember.

However, tempo is not the only aspect of music that is relevant in this respect. High-frequency sounds have been found to stimulate electrical activity in the brain, increasing alertness, and creating a state of mental readiness to store information. By contrast, low-frequency sounds are likely to make us feel sluggish and badly prepared for memorization.

Staging a Memory Concert

EXERCISE EIGHT

This exercise will help you to choose the music that you find conducive to memorization. Bear in mind the points about tempo and pitch opposite.

1. Look through your music collection and play various relaxing slow-tempo pieces that make you feel at ease with yourself. They might be pieces that have particular associations with past contentment.

2. Choose three pieces in particular as the core of your memory repertoire. Ideally, they should be pieces that you "melt into", enjoying the harmonies of the instruments. You could use vocal music too, so long as you do not find yourself too distracted by the words. Each piece should be at least five minutes long. Indian classical music can be particularly soothing, as can plainsong or Gregorian chant. Ultimately, of course, the choice is yours. Record your three pieces one after the other onto a single cassette.

3. Test the effectiveness of your memory music by a series of comparative experiments – for example, memorizing lists of random numbers, or street names from the telephone directory, or the order of playing cards in a randomly shuffled deck. Compare the relative effectiveness of each piece with the other two, and with silence.

The Art of Recall

We have looked in the preceding pages at of the vital factors of which we need to be aware if we wish to strengthen our memory skills – factors that form the basis of the specific memory techniques and systems described in the next chapter. We have also looked at ways to encourage the right context for effective memorization – in particular, the health aspects and (more tentatively) the use of music. It is now apt, in this survey of key principles, to switch our emphasis to the last stage of the memory process – recall.

The highest function of mind is its function of messenger.

D.H. Lawrence
1885–1930

Our brain holds far more information than we could ever access at any given time. However, memories are useless if they remain locked in some inner neurological recess. To have an effective memory, we need to be able to retrieve information at will – especially information that we have consciously placed in our mental store.

Our ability to retrieve memories depends largely on how we organized and stored them in the first place. If a memory was stored half-heartedly, without due concentration, or was not revised (see p.81), it may have faded away. Or if it was inappropriately filed, perhaps anchored by an ineffective association, like any misplaced article it may be difficult to locate. The art of recall is the skill by which we can make the appropriate link or series of links to lead us to the memories that we want to retrieve.

Recall is a strategic process. We initiate our mental search in a logical rather than a random fashion. And yet, as we use our left brain logically to sort through a sequence of options, our right brain works at a subliminal level (often through emotive and sensual associations) to help us complete the recall process successfully. For

example, if we're trying to remember the name of a town we visited last summer, we might first try to recapture the appearance or the sound of the name, and if these attempts fail we might try other logical approaches to the problem – "avenues" that we believe might lead us to the answer. So, we might bring to mind when we went, who we went with, how we travelled there. However, logic by itself will not be effective. As we travel down a promising avenue, we recall "creative" aspects of the event as well – the first view of the town from the road, the smell of lemon trees, the sound of singing crickets. Somehow, among these consciously invoked impressions, the name surfaces suddenly from the depths of memory – an experience with which we are all familiar. We may not even know which cue, or combination of cues, was responsible for this success.

Revisiting a conscious association to retrieve a memory is a not dissimilar process. Earlier in this chapter (p.72) we worked out a way to remember the name Horace Washington – by association with the poet and the city. As we think back to this character, an image of the city of Washington, DC might be the first thing that springs to mind, and then in a flash we might remember the classical link (the classical poet Horace, the neoclassical architecture), which then triggers the name itself – unfurling in the mind to the accompaniment of a silent cry of "eureka". Given the way in which the memory suddenly springs into the light of consciousness, why, we might ask, did we have to go through the palaver of circuitous association? The answer is that, as a name, Horace Washington meant nothing to us: it had no intrinsic associations, and so our chances of remembering it without artificial aids were small. But as soon as we wove a web of associations around the name, we hitched it to deep-rooted elements in our memory. These had already earned their keep in our memory banks. As we cast around in our mind for the answer, they acted, in a rapid succession of mental events, as a set of stepping stones to lead us to a point that we had visited only once before. By way of the familiar we reached the unfamiliar.

Memories may escape the action of the will, may sleep a long time, but when stirred by the right influence, though that influence be light as a shadow, they flash into full stature and life with everything in place.

John Muir
1916

Another aspect of recall is that the whole may be captured by means of a fragment. For example, if we are trying to remember the name of the breeding ground of the European and American eels, we might remember simply that there are four eel-like letters (s's) in the name – Sargasso Sea. Having recalled those four s's, which constitute a fragment of the whole name, we may find that the rest of the name rolls out in the mind automatically.

The environment in which we learn or experience something can itself be an effective retrieval cue. Psychologists call this phenomenon "context-dependent memory". When divers were given material to learn while underwater, in an experiment, they were able to recall the information far more comprehensively during their next dive than on dry land.

When a sight, sound or smell unexpectedly triggers apparently forgotten memories, this is called "surprise random recall". This type of unexpected recollection indicates that many more memories might be rediscovered if we could find the right triggers to bring them to consciousness.

Most of us have experienced what it is like to search in vain for a memory, using all the cues we can think of, only to find that the answer – perhaps the forgotten name of a politician or the title of a movie – springs to mind much later, when we least expect it. Faced with a difficult challenge, our brain has a lifetime of retrieval cues and associations to sort through, and sometimes a shift in focus, which gives our mental circuitry the time to do its rounds without experiencing the resistance of our frustration, can be all that is needed for the right information to turn up. When you begin memory training, try to bear in mind that you are beginning to formalize a process that your brain has been doing for you on its own all your life. Don't expect to tame the beast immediately – to master the art of recall requires patient trust, coupled with an understanding that answers cannot be forced.

CHAPTER FOUR

MEMORY WITH A MAP

Discovering memory techniques

We looked in the previous chapter at some key principles that lie behind the various techniques you can use to make your memory more effective – especially imagination, association and location. It is now time to explain the techniques themselves. Some of the approaches described over the following pages derive from age-old methods, adapted to modern requirements; some I have devised myself, and put into effect with gratifying success in the various World Memory Championships; some belong to a body of modern "folk knowledge", based largely on common sense. Think of this chapter as a basic toolkit. You may find some of the tools easier to use than others. There will certainly be items in the kit that you will want to modify to your own tastes and purposes – just as an artist might buy a set of commercial paints but add to them his or her own special mixes for favourite effects. My hope is that there is something here for everyone – I wish you success and revelation as you start to tap into the latent power of your brilliant mind.

1 2 3 4 5
1 2

Mnemonics

The word mnemonic (pronounced *nem-**on**-ik*) is derived from the Greek *mnemon*, meaning "mindful", which also gives us the name of the Greek goddess of memory Mnemosyne. A mnemonic is simply a device that helps us to remember something.

Although, strictly, the term applies to any memory technique, it is often used to denote specifically word-based techniques, especially acronyms or verses. However, word-based mnemonics do not meet with universal approval. Many academics dismiss them as exercises in idle wordplay, trivial ditties for parrots who want merely to echo a fact rather than to understand it. Some mnemonics are also rather slow to unravel. In my opinion, however, if a word-based mnemonic helps you to remember the right information at the right time, with a good chance of success, there is no harm in using it.

An *acronym* is a word made up of the initial letters of the words that you want to recall. For example, the acronym HOMES can remind you of the names of the five Great Lakes: Huron, Ontario, Michigan, Erie and Superior. But if you wanted to remember the lakes in size order (beginning with the largest), you might use the *extended acronym* Sergeant Major Hates Eating Onions.

How effective these techniques turn out to be depends, of course, on your natural ability to remember the acronyms or extended acronyms in the first place. However, if we take the trouble to make a few associations, these will help the brain to visualize in a creative form an otherwise bland list of data. So, perhaps the next time you need to recall the Great Lakes, you might expect that an image of, say, your house on the edge of a lake will spring to mind, reminding you of the acronym HOMES; or if you have to remember the lakes in order, you may be struck by the trigger-image of the Sergeant Major spitting out a cheese-and-onion sandwich, while out boating on a lake.

Rhythm can serve as an effective way to imprint information on the memory. This is why so many word-based mnemonics take the form of verses. How do you remember the number of days in each month? Many people use the rhyme "Thirty days hath September,/April, June and November." One of the "tidiest" rhymes (by pure coincidence) is that which helps us to remember the fate of each of King Henry VIII's wives, in order: "Divorced, Beheaded, Died,/Divorced, Beheaded, Survived."

Language in Numbers

In mathematics, the order of computation in complex equations is remembered by the acronym "Bless My Dear Aunt Sally!" – Brackets, Multiply, Divide, Add, Subtract.

Simple, word-based mnemonic devices can also be used to remember a sequence of numbers. Try creating your own mnemonic device to remember the first five decimal places of pi (3.14159). You might (as indeed many memorizers do) use the mnemonic whereby a sentence is constructed using words of the same number of letters as each digit in the sequence. For example, in the sentence "I have a super technique (to help me remember pi)," the number of letters in each word before the brackets is 14159.

This system may be slow when we come to recall the information but, as is the case with all mnemonics, if it works then it is worthwhile.

Visual Pegs

To prevent our deliberate memories – the items of information that we consciously commit to the process of absorb-and-recall – from drifting away, it helps to provide a way to anchor them in the flow. One of the most reliable methods depends particularly on association, but uses imagination and location (in its most rudimentary form) too. We mentally link our unit of information with a "landmark" that we will easily be able to locate in the mind, again and again. This serves as a visual peg or mailbox: we can revisit it at will. Two questions arise: how can we be sure of remembering the landmark? and how can we use this method to recall multiple items, such as a list of names, or a sequence of points to make in a speech or an interview?

These questions, in a sense, have the same answer. If we imagine not one peg but a whole set or system, the relationships between the pegs will help to fix them individually in our minds. As a simple way of grasping this point, think of a bird, a plane and a boomerang: to remember these three things, it helps to bear in mind that all of them have air as their natural element. A set or system gives a context to its components, and this context makes the components more memorable. If we remember three things out of four, the fourth thing is more easily recaptured if it is cousin to the other three.

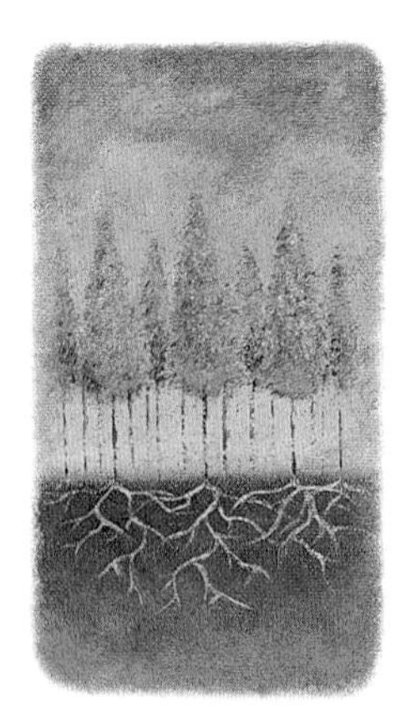

A system of visual pegs may in theory have any number of ingredients, although the number itself must be memorable, and therefore an even number is probably most appropriate: 10 is manageable; 20 is not infeasible.

The Memory Forest 10-note Keyboard

EXERCISE NINE

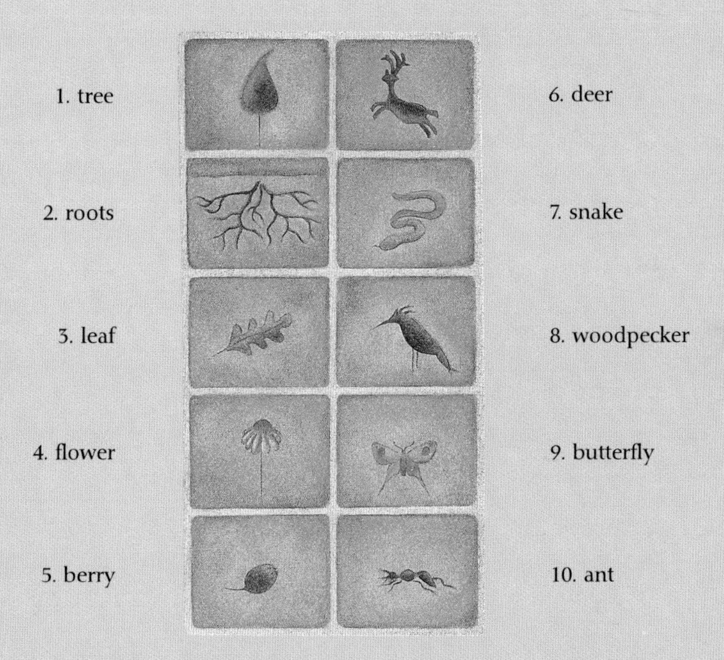

The memory forest keyboard consists of 10 logically ordered woodland features; each set of five (plants and animals) is arranged in size order.

1. Commit the keyboard to memory by visualizing it in sequence. One aid to memory is the logic behind the order of pegs: each set of five begins with the largest component and ends with the smallest (tree to berry; deer to ant); the plants and animals are easy to remember as a single set of 10 pegs, as they are linked by the element of the forest.

2. As an example use the keyboard to memorize the first 10 books of the Old Testament, in order: Genesis, Exodus, Leviticus, Numbers, Deuteronomy, Joshua, Judges, Ruth, 1 Samuel, 2 Samuel. Tree might remind you of family tree, showing the genesis of your family; roots are spread out under the ground, as if in exodus from the tree itself; for Leviticus you might think of a leaf "levitating" on a gentle breeze; and so on.

The Story Method

Memorizing through storytelling gives us an enjoyable opportunity to stretch our imagination. If you think back, you can probably recall many of the stories that you were told as a child – perhaps because they were dramatic, colourful, full of suspense and enjoyable, so that when you heard them you found them engaging.

In the peg system the pegs themselves are preselected, but in the story method the narrative comes into existence only by virtue of the items that we need to remember. To use this method, we string together in a tailor-made story a list of items or events that we wish to memorize. A new story is created for each new list, and it is memorable because we use our imagination to emphasize, exaggerate and elaborate in the way that all good storytellers do.

The principles are the same whether we are linking together items that have an intrinsic connection (such as the states of the US or kings and queens of England) or whether the items are completely unconnected (as in the exercise opposite). The links that we form between items must be sufficiently attention-holding – a dull link will result in poor recollection. To make your links interesting, employ such devices as the surreal, and movement and colour. For example, if the first two items in a list are "backpack" and "diamond", you might link them thus: "I was searching through my dirty backpack to find my dazzling diamond ring." Try not to fall into the trap of thinking that you will remember certain items without embellishing them: by making the items more vivid and your visualization of them precise (which includes imagining any sounds or smells they make), you will cement them in your mind.

Making a Memory Chain

EXERCISE TEN

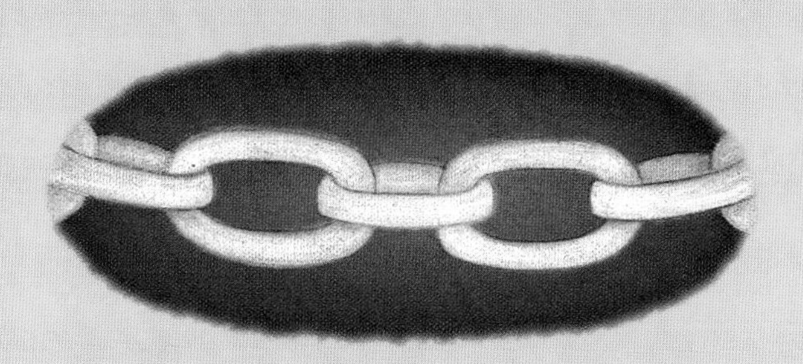

Use this exercise to train your mind to make effective links. The skills you acquire will help you get the most out of the story method.

1. Use this list of words: butter, crocodile, telephone, petrol, scissors, trousers, snow, cat, piano, suitcase. Think of a link to take you from butter to crocodile. Don't forget to use part-words if you find it easier (it may be more memorable to think of a slab of butter on a fragile piece of ***croc****kery, than butter being eaten by a* ***croc****odile; see p.100).*

2. Once you have made the first link, think about the context in which you have placed it. What is the setting? If you linked butter with crockery, you might imagine the scene in the kitchen. By keeping the location the same for the rest of the items, the links will be more memorable through the common bond of place.

3. Continue linking the words, one to the next. If one thing seems difficult to visualize in context, think about the details of the scene. For example, "snow" might be represented by a postcard on a kitchen noticeboard showing a snowcapped mountain; or the freezer compartment of your refrigerator might be filled with icy "snow".

4. Once you have finished forming the links, wait half an hour. Then, without looking at this page, try to recall all the items using the links you made. Note them down on a piece of paper, and then uncover the page to see how many you got right.

If you come across an item that you find hard to visualize (as you might if you needed to memorize, say, the states of the USA), you could try a system of "part-wording", in which you take the first or key syllable or syllables from the name of the item and make the necessary link using another word containing those same syllables. For example, if you had to link together Virginia and Washington, you might imagine your friend *Virginia* up to her eyeballs in soap-suds, *washing* the dishes.

This example is word-based, but equally we could follow an image-based system – where the items that we want to remember are given symbolic, visual form. For example, say we want to remember the signs of the zodiac, in their celestial order. First, we would look at the signs and their symbols because the symbols are immediately more memorable (and more visual) than the names (Aries the ram, Taurus the bull, Gemini the twins, and so on). Then, we would begin to formulate a story beginning with the image of a ram. Remember that the best stories have a beginning, a middle and an end, and are full of suspense and action. Try to be as creative as you can; tell the tale out loud to an imaginary audience if it helps, use pace and tone to enliven the story. We might imagine that we are standing in a field that stretches as far as the eye can see. Suddenly over the horizon comes a ram, running at top speed toward us. Just as we are about to run out of the way, we hear the thunderous rhythm of hooves and realize that the ram is running in order to escape the charge of a bull. As the bull comes over the horizon, the steamy breath from its nostrils puffing angrily into the air, we see that sitting on top of it, two small figures – twins – are screaming for help ... and so on.

Now try the exercise on p.99 (to help you form links in a list of unconnected items) and the one opposite (connected items).

Weaving a Narrative Spell

EXERCISE ELEVEN

Creating a story is a personal act – for the story to be memorable, it has to follow a sequence of events that you can imagine vividly. Try creating a narrative to help you remember the order of the planets outward from the Sun. Adapt the basic method given here for other information also.

1. The sequence of the planets is Mercury, Venus, Earth, Mars, Jupiter, Saturn, Uranus, Neptune, Pluto. Visualize the planets, giving each a form to reflect its associations – Mercury might be a thermometer; Venus, a beautiful woman, like the goddess.

2. Think of a setting for your story. Will it take place in space or on Earth? If on Earth, whereabouts? Imagine the opening scene in detail – what is the landscape like? are there people present? what is the weather like? what noises are there? Begin to weave the narrative out of this scene – what part does the first planet play?

3. Work the remaining planets, in order, into your story. Be creative. One planet represents a character (Venus?); another, a place (Earth?); another, an animal (Pluto?).

4. When you have finished, wait an hour and test yourself. Using the story as a guide, can you recall the planets in order? Were any of the links too weak? If so, rethink them.

The Journey Method

The journey method combines the peg method with the story method. Each of these latter two methods uses two of the three keys to memory – imagination and association. The journey method takes things one step further and uses location too. For this reason, I believe that the journey method is the most powerful of all mnemonic techniques.

The method is based on a fixed, preplanned, mental route along which is a set number of stages to act as anchors for the pieces of data that we need to memorize. When a memory is fixed by association following the peg method, there is always a risk that the link will be too weak to be readily recaptured. However, with the journey method the links in the chain are much stronger because the stages in the journey are linked by the predetermined geography of the route itself, and each piece of information to be remembered is "pegged" to a fixed landmark on that route.

I am an enthusiastic golfer, and I often hear the journey method being used in the clubhouse by other golfers – without their even knowing it – to deliver a blow-by-blow account of their games. They remember perfectly every hole played: what clubs they and their opponents chose, how many strokes were played, the number of putts, and so on. What they recall is a highly complex list of numerical data. All of a sudden every golfer in the clubhouse is a memory wizard – why? The journey method. Each golfer has used a mental route consisting of 18 stages around the golf course. At each stage they have stationed specific facts about their

game. When they mentally retrace their steps, the golfers recall, by association, the details stored along the journey.

We might think that the ease with which the information is recalled is altogether unsurprising – and in many ways we would be right. It is completely logical. We all use the journey method from time to time, whether we are trying to recall a game of golf or trying to remember whereabouts in the grocery store we can find some eggs. When the items of information actually belong to the context of the journey, it is obvious that mentally "walking" the route will bring us to the data that we need. However, what I have come to realize is that unrelated pieces of information can be placed along the same journey (say, the golf course or grocery store) and that they too can be retrieved by mentally retracing our steps. Really all I did was recognize something that we all do naturally, and I began to use it with purpose.

So how do we choose our journey? Any familiar route will do – the important thing is that the stages or landmarks are memorably distinctive. Spend a few moments now thinking about a journey that you have made many times – perhaps the journey each morning from home to work; or the trip from your own home to your parents'. It might even be a journey from childhood, such as a walk through the woods or to school. Perhaps, like me, you might decide to mentally walk your favourite golf course. Whatever the journey, visualize each stage in as much detail as you can. If your chosen journey is the walk from your house to the local store, imagine standing at your front door ready to leave. Visualize yourself walking out through the porch, down the path to the front gate, then from the front gate, turning right and walking down the road. What do you pass? Imagine every building or landmark that you pass in as much detail as you can. If it is a building, what is the architecture like? What happens inside? If it is a store, for example, what does it sell? Who owns it? Perhaps it is a bakery and the smell of freshly baked bread wafts along the streets. Think of every landmark in three dimensions. How does your perspective change as you pass each one?

Could any of the landmarks act as fixed stages at which to post items that you want to memorize? Obviously, the more striking they are, the better – try to include as many as possible that stand out as being especially distinctive (perhaps a war memorial or a dilapidated factory). The number of stages will determine the number of items that you will be able to post on this particular journey – so if you have 24 stages in your journey, then you can place 24 items of a shopping list, 24 points of a speech, or 24 people

Walking the Walk

EXERCISE TWELVE

If at first you find it difficult to recall the items that you placed along a journey, this exercise will train your mind to make strong associations by asking you actually to "walk the walk".

1. Choose a journey that is short enough for you to walk – perhaps a stroll in a favourite park. Before you go, visualize the walk and decide upon 10 stages along it. They might include a favourite bench, the rose garden, a children's play area or a pond.

2. Write the following list on a piece of paper: wheel, explosion, gorilla, car, bishop, pencil, cage, blue, computer, champagne. Take the list, go out and "walk the walk".

3. When you arrive at the first stage, stand still. Make an imaginative association to link this stage with the first item on the list. Walk on, linking all the items to all the stages.

4. When you return home replay the walk in your mind, thinking again about what items you linked to what stages. Refer to the list of items if you need to.

5. The next day do the walk again, this time without the written list. As you come to each stage, recall the item that you mentally placed there. Then, on the following day, replay the walk only in your imagination – can you remember all the items?

in a room. But don't expect too much of yourself at first – start with around 10 stages.

To put the journey method into practice we place the items that we need to remember along our chosen route, by visualizing an association, a scene or tableau is created in the mind's eye. Say you needed to remember a list of famous actors, how might you position each person memorably at the appropriate landmark? For example, Clint Eastwood might be leaning on your garden gate dressed as a cowboy, blowing smoke from the barrel of a gun. However, the more imaginative your postings, the more memorable they will be. So perhaps, instead of simply providing a leaning post for the movie star, your garden gate becomes a pair of saloon doors. You might imagine that Clint comes bursting through them with his cowboy swagger – the street falls silent as he does so. By the time you are finished, your journey will be populated in a surreal way by larger-than-life actors doing the things typical of them. For example, Johnny Weissmuller, who played Tarzan in the 1930s, might be swinging from the church spire, making his famous animal call.

Of course, there's no reason why we should call upon only one journey. I keep a store of different journeys (like a series of mental videotapes), each of which I use to memorize certain types of information: my golf course to memorize a deck of cards; a journey I made as a child to memorize the names of people at conferences I attend. If I need to remember a shopping list, I place the items on a journey around my house. In effect, this is an extension of the Roman "memory villa" technique. Like the Romans, who created mental pictures of their own homes, I believe the journey method works best if the journey takes place in a setting that we know.

The Memory House

EXERCISE THIRTEEN

This exercise is the basis for memorizing 10 grocery items by depositing them along a journey around the home. You can adapt it for other items.

1. Visualize the inside of your home. Imagine walking around its rooms from its main entrance to the kitchen, the lounge, the dining room, and so on, finishing in your bedroom.

2. Establish 10 stages around the house at which you could place items that you wish to remember: the mirror in the entrance hall, the sink in the kitchen, the bedside table, and so on. Visualize the stages in the order in which you come across them.

3. Mentally walk around your home, placing each of the following items in the correct order: cheese, milk, oranges, ice cream, cereal, bananas, bread, broccoli, fish, tomatoes. Be imaginative – the cheese is draped like a coat over the hall chair, the milk is running out of the taps in the kitchen sink, a tomato forms the base of your bedside lamp.

4. Wait for an hour or so, and then imagine retracing your steps. As you come to each stage, the item that you placed there should come to mind. When you go to the grocery store, recall the mental journey around your house and don't forget a single item!

The Dominic System

The difficulty with trying to remember numbers is that they have little significance outside their own abstract world. To overcome this, I developed the DOMINIC (Decipherment Of Mnemonically Interpreted Numbers Into Characters) system as a way of linking numbers to the stimulating and far more memorable world outside.

At the heart of the DOMINIC system is your imagination, which is used to develop a way of "seeing" numbers as images (it can provide an alternative or a complement to the number-shape system described on pp.110–11). By far the most successful images for this purpose are those of people, because they are flexible, mobile and reactive – elements that the DOMINIC system uses to aid recall.

So how does the system work? First, I think of numbers that have automatic associations with people (for me, at least). For example, 07 becomes James Bond (whose agent number is 007), 10 becomes Dudley Moore (star of the film *10*), and 39 becomes the "memory man" (from John Buchan's novel *The Thirty-Nine Steps*). However, for those numbers without immediate associations it is necessary to build mental stepping stones linking number to image, and this is done through a 10-letter alphabet. To each of the 10 digits (0, 1, 2, 3, 4, 5, 6, 7, 8, 9) ascribe a letter; for 1 you might use A, the first letter of the alphabet, with B for 2 and C for 3, and so on. However, it is often better to mix logical connections with creative ones:

zero might be linked to the letter O, purely because of its shape, and 6 to the letter S (because "six" has two *s* sounds).

The next step is to group numbers into pairs, which are then used to create the initials of people. For the single digits between 0 and 9, this means placing a zero before them (01, 02, 03 and so on). 00 represents zero itself. Thereafter, obviously, the numbers up to and including 99 have two digits. So, 66 might become S(ylvester) S(tallone) and 12 A(nne) B(oleyn). The choice of people needs to be as diverse as possible. It is not necessary to be able to form a fully realized mental picture of each person, but it is important to be able to associate them with their own characteristic action or prop: Stallone with a machine gun, Anne Boleyn with decapitation. Out of this a vocabulary begins to emerge, which you will then need to expand to cover all the numbers from zero to 99. This may at first seem a daunting task, but if you set yourself a target of creating personas for 20 numbers a week, it is surprising how quickly you can become fluent in this new language. The key is to ensure that the associations are obvious.

Therefore, to remember a medical-insurance number (say, 071237) think of a location, such as your local surgery. Break the number up into pairs and assign letters (and in turn characters and actions) according to your interpretation of the DOMINIC system: 07 is James Bond/racing a car, 12 becomes A(nne) B(oleyn)/decapitation, 37 becomes C(laudia) S(chiffer)/on the catwalk. Then put a mini-story together, using a system of person-action-person-action. Thus, 071237 becomes a scene in the surgery in which James Bond (person) decapitates (action) Claudia Schiffer (person). If you have a single digit left after pairing the numbers (say, if the number in this example had been 0712374), combine the DOMINIC system with the number-shape system.

The Number-Shape System

The modern world is full of numbers intended to make our lives easier. We have to remember PIN numbers for our bank cards, security access codes for the buildings in which we work, and parental censoring numbers for our televisions – let alone the phone numbers of our friends, family, colleagues and clients. If we leave our personal organizer or address book at home – or worse still, lose it – we feel totally lost. Time to reinstate the only personal organizer that we can never lose: our brain.

The problem with memorizing numbers is that to those of us without a great passion for arithmetic they provide little inspiration. They are static, inexpressive and impersonal. On the face of it, they relate only to the logical part of our brains. To make them more memorable, we have to give them appeal for our creative side too – we have to make them fluid, visual and imaginative.

One of the most popular methods is the number-shape system in which each number between and including zero and 9 is turned into a particular item that relates to the numeral's written shape. For example, 0 (zero) may be seen as a golden ring or a football; 1 may be a candle or a pencil; 2, a swan or a snake; 3, lips in profile or a pair of handcuffs; 4, the sail of a yacht, or a flag; 5, a seahorse or a hook; 6, an elephant's trunk or a golf club; 7 a boomerang or a diving board; 8, a snowman or an hourglass; and 9, a balloon on a ribbon. You can choose your own associations – try to make them relevant to your life by including items from your favourite hobbies and so on.

Once the associations are made, we can create stories by which to remember sequences of numbers. For example, if your bank-card PIN number is 4291, you might imagine that to get to your bank you have to sail (4) down a river, passing a swan (2), which holds in its beak a ribbon on the end of which is a balloon (9). Tied to the other end of the ribbon is a pencil (1) – you take it to sign your name.

For longer sequences, try using the journey method (see pp.102–7) combined with the number-shape system. So, if the first three numbers in a sequence of 12 are 8, 0 and 3 and our journey is one along a golf course, we might imagine a snowman at the first tee (stage one in the journey); a golden ring glistening at the bottom of the tin cup of the first hole (stage two); a golfer trying to swing a club while wearing handcuffs at the next tee (stage three); and so on.

Here, where we reach the sphere of mathematics, we are among processes which seem to some the most inhuman of all human activities and the most remote from poetry. Yet it is here that the artist has the fullest scope of his imagination.

Havelock Ellis
1923

Remembering the Hundreds

We can use a combination of the DOMINIC system and the number-shape system to remember numbers in the hundreds. All we have to do is break down the three-digit number into a pair of digits and a single figure. For example, 150 becomes 15-0. According to the DOMINIC system 15 is AE, while in the number-shape system 0 might be remembered as a football. In order to memorize the number 150, we combine the two systems. So, perhaps Albert Einstein (AE) is kicking a football. And what if you want to remember that your friend lives at house number 125? 12 is AB in the DOMINIC system, so you might think of Anne Boleyn. In the number-shape system, 5 is a seahorse. Anne Boleyn is wearing huge seahorse-shaped earrings and sitting on the front porch of your friend's house.

Mind Maps

Mind Maps were invented by Tony Buzan, who has written or co-authored 80 bestsellers on the brain and learning and is co-founder of the Mind Sports Olympiad. A Mind Map can be seen as a physical representation of information to be held in the memory – just as the journey method is a mental representation. Mind Maps are highly effective aids to recording and retaining data because they reduce subjects to their key points, giving you a summary of fundamental knowledge that you can hold in your mind's eye. All you need is a sheet of paper and ideally a set of coloured pencils or pens.

A Mind Map can be imagined as an overhead view of a tree with branches that grow only from the sides of the trunk, not upward. It has a central image which represents the subject matter of the map. Lines (referred to as "branches") are drawn radiating from this central element, each branch representing a main theme. Ideally, each of these branches is drawn in a particular colour. Each theme is represented by a single sketch labelling the relevant branch. Then, key words to represent related pieces of information are written (or represented pictorially) along further lines (sub-branches) drawn from each of the main branches. Ideally, all the lines attached to one main branch should be drawn in the same colour, so that groups of information are immediately recognizable. The lines go on branching off, becoming smaller as increasingly specific details are noted.

To create a Mind Map – for example, of this book – take a large piece of paper and begin with a central image. You might draw a picture of a head and label it "Memory". Each branch should have only one key word or phrase – for example, "History" or

"Brain" – and each should have its own distinctive colour. Draw symbolic images alongside to serve as memory aids. From each main branch, draw sub-branches and label them with appropriate topics – for example, "Storytellers" and "Greeks" from the "History" branch. If an associated thought springs to mind, note it down and draw a line connecting it to the relevant branch.

One advantage of Mind Maps is that they provide a way to impose a coherent shape on knowledge that grows randomly, according to the thoughts we have and the information that we pick up. No matter how complex the Mind Maps, there will always be an appropriate place for any new element you wish to add. The Mind Map, as it grows in this way, both aids and reflects your evolving understanding of the subject.

CHAPTER FIVE

MEMORY IN ACTION

Memory techniques for everyday life

Most of us would not find it difficult to be specific about the ways in which a better memory would improve our lives on a day-to-day basis. To be able accurately to put a name to a face, to recall instantly a friend's telephone number or address, to remember information at a moment's notice, to keep a mental diary of anniversaries and never to be lost for the *mot juste* – such skills become available to anyone willing to try some new approaches to memory. In this chapter we look at techniques for all these daily tasks, as well as for playing card games and chess to win, and effective speechmaking without notes. Quite simply, we look at particular applications of memory in our lives – we may be surprised to learn how great the potential is for enhancing the pleasure we take in doing something well.

Matching Names and Faces

Most of us tend to be able to recognize a face that we have seen before. What we find difficult is remembering the name that goes with it. One of the most pleasing everyday benefits of an improved memory is the ability to match names and faces after only a brief introduction – even if that introduction was several years ago.

The key is to link together the face, name and place in a chain of association. When you are introduced to someone, study their face. Are there any distinguishing features? If you were to create a caricature of the face, what parts would you exaggerate? Does the face look warm or cold; happy or sad; vital or tired; confident or shy? Ethically, of course, making judgments based on appearance is highly dubious. However, studies have shown that subjects asked to make personality assumptions purely on someone's "look" benefitted from greatly improved recall of that person's name. For the purposes of your own memory, lay the ethical question aside (but don't let your judgments influence the impressions you form about the person). How might anything that occurs to you about the person or their features reflect their name? Say you are introduced to a woman called Valerie Nightingale. She has a happy face, pointed nose and soft voice. You might visualize a beautiful bird swooping into a valley, singing happily. The valley triggers the name Valerie and, as the nightingale is a bird famous for its "voice", the birdsong triggers the memory of her surname; the pointed nose reinforces the bird idea. Condense the image: visualize the bird nesting in her hair. When you come to recall her name, her face will prompt the image of the bird in her hair, thus triggering the chain of association.

There are mystically in our faces certain characters which carry in them the motto of our souls, wherein he that cannot read A, B, C may read our natures.

Sir Thomas Browne
1642

What's in a Name?

EXERCISE FOURTEEN

This exercise will give you practice in forming images and associations that will help you remember names and faces. To simulate a first meeting, do the exercise with a friend.

1. From a pile of magazines and newspapers, cut out 10 pictures of unfamiliar faces for each of you. If the photos don't have captions to identify them, make up appropriate names and write them on the backs of the pictures.

2. Swap your pictures with those your friend has cut out and named. Lay them out and study the faces before checking the names. Work on your initial impressions. What might the person do for a living? Is the face pleasant, stern, time-worn, jovial, anxious, mischievous, and so on? Where might the person live?

3. Let your imagination form associations between the faces and the names. Limit the time you spend doing this to less than a minute for each face.

4. Put the pictures to one side and wait for about fifteen minutes, or longer if you like. Test your partner by showing them the photos and covering up the names. Ask your partner to test you. How many names did you recall correctly?

Keeping a Date

Imagine if, month by month, you could trust yourself to remember all the birthdays and other anniversaries you need to acknowledge and could see them looming as the date approaches; and if you could also recall the dates for business meetings or deadlines at work. Imagine too that you can do this without having to rely upon pieces of paper, a diary or an assistant. Socially, you would be able to respond immediately when someone asks you if you want to meet up with them next week; you would always make your partner feel special by not having to be reminded about your most important anniversary; and in business you would impress clients and employers alike with your mental reference of schedules.

Memory is the diary that we all carry about with us.

Oscar Wilde
1895

You can use the journey method to construct a mental monthly planner that will help you remember important dates. The basic idea is to allocate each key event to up to 31 stages in a preselected journey (see exercise, right) – each stage representing a day of the month. Of course, there will be some days that will need to have more than one piece of information attached – perhaps two meetings in an afternoon or a day when two friends share a birthday. In such cases, you will need to use your imagination. You could imagine a meeting with a surreal hybrid agenda – if one meeting is about money and the other about quality control, you might conjure up in your mind a damaged banknote. Or you might visualize the two friends together at the same event – what would be the chemistry between them? As always with the more elaborate memory systems, they are most effective if you experiment and adapt until you have a working method in which you believe.

Using a Mental Diary

EXERCISE FIFTEEN

This exercise will help you to create your mental monthly planner.

1. Choose a journey with 31 stages – each stage represents a day of the month (it does not matter that some months will fall short of the entire journey). Try to begin at a high point, such as the top of a hill, where you can easily survey the route, and so the month ahead.

2. Reinforce the midpoint of the month (15th) by giving it a particularly unique or interactive attribute – perhaps the stage is marked by a ladder that you have to climb or a stream that you have to jump across. This will make it easier for you to pinpoint your "current" position in relation to the rest of the month.

3. Distil each appointment into a single symbol – perhaps your anniversary is symbolized by your partner using an outsized wedding ring as a "hula hoop". Place each symbol at the relevant stage of the journey. Try to make the symbols and stages interact. If a meeting with your boss is on the 4th, say, and the fourth stage is a belltower, you might imagine your boss swinging about on a bell rope. At the end of each month, visualize wiping clean the stages, and post any prearranged appointments for the new month.

Finding the Right Word

The international network of readers on the Oxford World Reading Programme collect around 18,000 new words and idioms every month – in English alone. Add this to the existing words and phrases in the English language, and is it any wonder that sometimes we feel unable to come up with the description for something?

There are various techniques aimed at bringing to mind a word, but one of the simplest is to work from the beginning of the alphabet, trying each letter in turn, until you feel that you have hit upon the right one to start the word. Once you think that you may have found the letter, roll it around your tongue, speaking it out loud. See if the word naturally unfurls. If it does not and if the word begins with a consonant, try each vowel after the letter to try to tempt out the rest of the word. If it begins with a vowel, your task of experimenting with all the consonants will, of course, be more laborious.

Another way to recall a word might be to start off, aloud, a number of different sentences which need for you to express the required meaning. As you begin each sentence, have faith that your buried knowledge of the word will resurface.

In remembering words, it helps if we know the etymology or derivation – the units of sense (often modified from Latin or Greek) from which historically words are built up. However, our own, invented key etymology can be just as useful. Often a key syllable will conjure up the word's meaning. For example, when committing to memory the word "amortize" (meaning to recover the cost of investment), we might think of *mort* (the French for "death") as a murdered or eliminated cost.

Crossword Heaven

EXERCISE SIXTEEN

A quick crossword can be a frustrating pastime if the answers to those last few clues lie just beyond reach. Try using the ideas below to fill in the gaps and complete your puzzle – without referring to a dictionary!

1. When you have some letters filled in already, write them out in order on a clean piece of paper, leaving spaces for blanks (don't draw lines to indicate blanks). Look at the part-complete word. Try not to stare: soften your focus and imagine looking "through" it to the other side of the paper. Then, as you bring your gaze back into focus, bear the clue in mind, as your view becomes sharp, to fill in the blanks. Does the word appear?

2. Alternatively, try using a system of placement to bring an answer to mind. Think about the clue. Have you ever talked to anyone about the subject? For example, if the clue is "Stick passed in relay race (5)," think back to a conversation you had about, say, the Olympics. Who was the conversation with? Where were you? Hopefully, thinking around the subject will reveal the word you need (in this example, "baton").

3. Or, a solution's elusiveness could mean that you are attributing the wrong structure to it. For example, the syllable "s?y" might have a consonant in the middle (sly) rather than a vowel (say). Try alternative structures to see if the word springs into being.

Making Speeches

I never could make a good impromptu speech without several hours to prepare for it.

Mark Twain
1879

Making speeches can strike fear into the hearts of the best of us. Even actors, comedians, lawyers, priests, politicians and many others who regularly speak in public will confess to becoming nervous before a "performance". However, if we have confidence in our memory, have organized the speech well and can devise a trigger system that will set off our first and subsequent thoughts, then speech-nerves can become a thing of the past.

Used appropriately, the journey method (see pp.102–7) can provide one of the best ways to effectively memorize a speech. Firstly, it provides a pre-established "first thought" (the starting post of the journey, removing the tension about recalling the first words of the speech). But, more importantly, it creates a logical, visual system by which we are able to anchor all the main points of what we want to say.

If you are unaccustomed to making speeches, spend some time establishing the content and ensuring that it will be logical, coherent and imaginative – this in itself will make it more memorable for you. Use a Mind Map to help organize the main points you want to make. Then, write a paragraph about each point, making sure that your argument follows a clear logic. You might ask a friend to read through it and make suggestions. Once your speech is written, read it twice in its complete form so that you are completely familiar with it.

Decide what journey will act as the framework of your speech. You may pick a trip that is related to the event at which you are making the speech (if you are the best man at your friend's wedding, you might choose the walk between your house and his or a hike you once did together). Mentally run through the journey a few times – ideally choose one that you already use – and establish the stages at which you will come to the points in your speech.

Now refer back to the Mind Map that you made before writing out your speech. Visualize each key point as a single, highly creative image. If the first point in your best man's speech is that the bride and groom met on a fishing trip, you might visualize two fish dressed in wedding outfits dancing. Use your senses. What do they smell like? What noises do their fins make as they dance?

Once you have created a visualization for each point in the speech, mentally walk your journey, depositing the visualizations in order at the established stages on the route. Try to make the image interact with the setting. For example, if the first stage in your journey is the front porch of your home, perhaps you have to push past the dancing "fish" to get down your path. Imagine reciting the words of the speech between the stages.

Play the journey over to yourself in this way at least five times: one hour after you have devised it; the next day; and then at regular intervals until the big day. According to the revision rule of five (whereby repeating something five times commits it permanently to memory), the speech should now be unforgettable, and along with it the triggers that will allow you to give a scintillating and confident talk. However, if when you stand up to start speaking, you still feel fearful, take a deep breath. Close your eyes and imagine yourself at the start of your journey. Take your first mental step, open your eyes and talk. The rest will come naturally.

Memory and Games

According to convention, each square on the chess board is designated a number and a letter. Numbers (one through eight) run up the side of the board and letters (a through h) run from left to right. White begins play in rows one and two; black in seven and eight.

(The "pieces" – that is all the chessmen except the pawns – are given letters: Queen, Q; King, K; Knight, N; Rook, R; Bishop, B.)

We learned in the DOMINIC system (see p.108) to designate letters to numbers (1=A; 2=B; and so on). As each square on the board can be identified by a number and a letter, this code can easily be converted to initials (and so to a persona). Perhaps white's first move is knight to c3 (Nc3). Using the DOMINIC system, c3 = CC (say, Charlie Chaplin), so the knight moves to Charlie Chaplin.

But how is this memorable? It isn't – yet. Each chess piece also needs a persona. Select characters who seem to "match" the pieces. Perhaps the queens are Elizabeth II; the knights, Sir Lancelot of the Round Table; and so on. You only need one character for each type of piece (you will need to devise a system whereby you can recall which of your knights moves to a square that either could reach; similarly for the rooks). The pawns do not need characters – you'll know a pawn's move as it involves only the square's persona.

In the previous example, Nc3 gives us Lancelot (the knight) moving to Charlie Chaplin (square c3). To remember the *sequence* of play, we need to deposit each move at the stages of a journey. So, if Nc3 is white's opening move, first we combine the two personae into a single image: Lancelot adopts the action or prop of Charlie Chaplin (Lancelot jousting with Chaplin's cane?). Then we place this image at stage one of the journey. Black's response (placed at stage two) might be Nf6 – Lancelot singing like Frank Sinatra (in the DOMINIC system, six is given the letter "s"). A 12-stage journey will enable you to memorize an opening gambit; 60 stages, perhaps a whole game!

One of the most effective uses of memory in games is for cards. The box (below) puts memory techniques for blackjack into practice. However, if you are gambling, beware! – no system is infallible.

Learning to memorize a randomly shuffled deck of cards is a good way generally to exercise your memory. "Speed Cards" (memorizing a deck against the clock) is my favourite of all the heats in the Memory Championships. The following is the technique I use.

Turning the Tables

A whole book could be written on cardcounting, but here's a brief summary of my technique. In blackjack, the greater the concentration of high cards left in the dealer's "shoe", the better the cards to come. To remember which cards have been dealt, I give each card played a numerical value. Cards two through six = 1; seven through nine = 0; and 10, ace and the court cards = –1. I keep a running total of the values of played cards. Bets must be placed before each deal, so if the total is greater than +1, I know that high cards are still in the shoe and I increase my next bet; and vice versa. This technique is good for a single deck, but casinos use four to eight decks of cards in a shoe, so a "true" count can be gained only by dividing the running total by the approximate number of whole decks left to play.

First, we must apply the three keys of memory – imagination, association and location – in the form of the journey method. A familiar route of 52 stages will provide a mental videotape on which to record the chance order of all the cards in the deck. The journey should be especially familiar. Before you even pick up a deck, think carefully about the journey and establish precisely the 52 landmarks. Run the "tape" of them through your mind over and over until they are fixed.

Finally, pick up a deck of cards. If you are to be able to remember these cards in any order, each card needs its own permanent and unique visual code. Translate each card into a person – people can interact with the stages in the journey, so they are memorable. Pick out the court cards and examine the faces. Imagine that each is a person known to you – perhaps the Jack of Hearts resembles your nephew in some way. If the court cards do not remind you of anyone you actually know, give them the persona of someone famous.

Next, translate each of the other cards into a person. This is more difficult, but once you have mastered this particular part of the code, memorizing the deck will become straightforward – if not, to begin with, easy. Choose an appropriate letter for each suit: H for Hearts; C for Clubs; D for Diamonds; and S for Spades. Use the DOMINIC system to give each number from 1 to 10 a letter. Having attributed letters to suits and letters to numbers, every card has a two-letter code: the five of diamonds is ED; the two of clubs BC; and so on. Use these letters as the initials of a person – either someone you know or someone famous. For example, ED might be a friend with these initials, while BC might be Bill Clinton. You do not have to stick rigidly to the DOMINIC system: if the ace of hearts is more memorable as your partner, then so be it! Use your imagination – create a set of visualizations that will excite a powerful subjective response.

Memorizing Cards of Chance

EXERCISE SEVENTEEN

Using the letter–number system explained in the text opposite, memorize your first randomly shuffled deck of cards, then test your accuracy.

1. Run through your 52-stage journey, just to double-check that it is firmly set in your mind. Then, quickly flick through the deck of cards without intending to memorize the order, but simply reminding yourself of the person with whom you associate each card.

2. Shuffle the deck. Then, take a deep breath, focus and turn the first card face up. Imagine the person whom the card represents at the first stage in your journey. Give them an action or prop – if it is Bill Clinton, perhaps he is waving the US flag.

3. Continue to turn the cards slowly, one on top of the other, mentally placing each "person" along your journey. Take your time. Once you have been through the deck, replay the journey in your mind and note down all the people you remember. Decipher your code back into playing cards. Check your notes against the deck. Don't worry if you've made mistakes – practice makes perfect! At the next attempt, time yourself.

Memory at School

Very few schools devote lessons to teaching how to learn – even though it would make the lives of students and teachers immensely easier. This is why I felt it important to include in this book a few paragraphs dedicated to memory techniques for effective learning.

The basic principles of memory can be applied to all kinds of teaching and learning, whatever your age. Once you have proved to yourself that you can memorize a list of 10 or 20 unconnected words using a memory chain (see p.97), the journey method (see pp.102–7) or any other method that appeals to you, it becomes easy to see how you can apply the same techniques to many academic subjects.

How might you use imagination and association to form links that will help you to memorize the capital cities of all the US states? For example, the capital of Texas is Austin, so perhaps you visualize an *aust*ere Texan standing over you. On his head is an outsized oil-baron's hat, with a wide band – this helps you to remember Texas because you know it is famous for oil production.

Likewise, linguistic mnemonics can help us to remember any number of facts and figures, including the dates of historical events (such as when Columbus landed in the New World: "In fourteen hundred and ninety-two, Columbus sailed the ocean blue") and even scientific subjects, such as biology and chemistry. For example, the three enzymes in the body that convert starch and glycogen to sugars are amylase, tripase and lipase. What mnemonic can might help you remember the names of the enzymes? You might think of your friend Amy, who always stumbles over her words: "*Amy trip*ped over her *lip*."

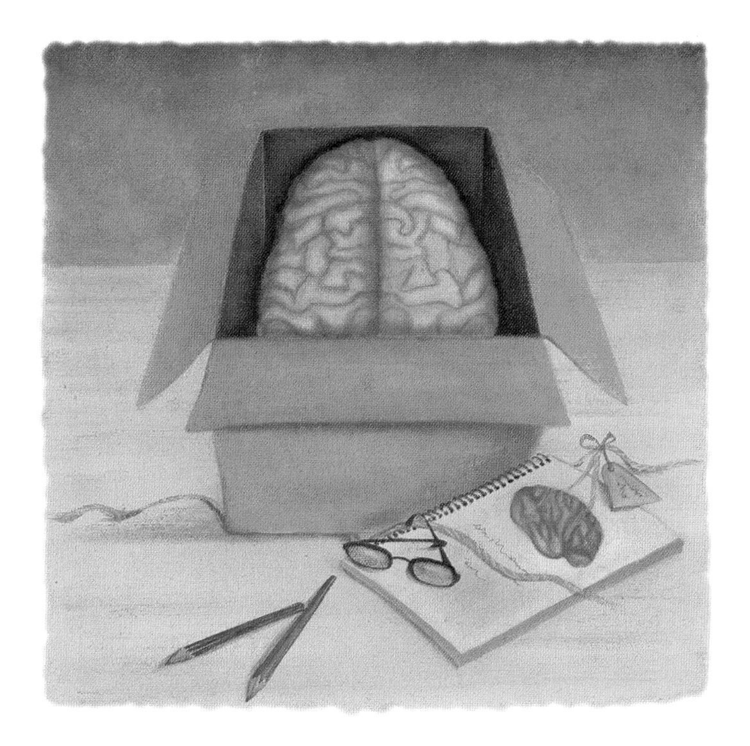

Try using the number-shape system (see pp.110–11) to remember tables of information or the atomic numbers of chemical elements. For example, the atomic number for carbon is six, so we may see an elephant's trunk (the image we have chosen to represent the number six) stoking the coals on a fire (coal, of course, is carbon), or we could visualize an elephant holding a carbon pencil in its trunk as it tries to do its chemistry homework.

Memory techniques transcend language barriers, so they can also be used to remember foreign words when we are learning a new language. For example, if we wanted to remember that the Italian word for a stamp is *francobollo*, we might form a mini-story and imagine how amazed we would be if, out of the blue, we were *stamp*eded by a *bull* called *Frank*!

Reading and Retaining

The advantage of learning from books, journals, reports and so on is that we can work at our own pace. We have ultimate control over how much material to present to our brains for retention, and how much time to allow. We can also be selective, choosing to ignore information if we find it unhelpful. The disadvantage is that we lose the impact of someone else's presentation – animation, verbal emphasis and visual stimulation. Reading to learn is an effort because the only stimulation we receive is from the words themselves.

This point highlights the significance of intrinsic interest: the financial analysis for this year's AGM might strike a leaden chord. So what can we do to be sure of retaining whatever we select from our reading, no matter what the subject matter?

In the absence of any other visual stimulus (there will on occasions be illustrations) we rely upon our imaginations to create impact. But before embarking on the challenge, *plan your reading*. Evaluate the material so that you do not waste time reading surplus data or opinions. Feeling duty-bound to read something from cover to cover will only result in a sense of your being burdened by the pages ahead, and will probably mean that you concentrate more on notching up pages than on content. Try to read actively, not passively: *question the logic* behind every statement. Playing an active role during reading will greatly enhance your understanding and therefore your memory. Finally, *animate and review* the information by drawing a Mind Map (see pp.112–13), or at least by writing up a list of brief cues in the form of names and topics, of the key points.

Evaluate, Assimilate, Remember

EXERCISE EIGHTEEN

Retaining information from our reading, especially on subjects that are of marginal interest, requires an overall strategy.

1. Make a list of 3–5 questions, the answers to which you expect to find in the text. This will give your reading clear objectives. If, say, you intend to read about the American War of Independence, you might ask: when did this take place? how did it start? who were the major players on both sides? how was the conflict resolved?

2. Check the contents of the book or journal for clues as to where essential information lies. Then, scan the index, noting down references to topics that you need to cover in order to answer your questions. Concentrate only on these page references.

3. Each paragraph will normally have a "topic sentence" which summarizes its central point. Pay these sentences particular attention, as well as any crucial names, terms, dates and formulae. Trace the logic of the argument. Could you reproduce this logic in a debate?

4. Draw a Mind Map. From the central image, draw lines outward for each theme. From these draw lines for topic sentences. Keep going until you have an instant reference chart.

Speed Reading

Speed reading is not only about being able to run our eyes quickly over a page, it is also about being able to store that information quickly – in a sense it is "speed memorizing" too. Some people believe that reading slowly, paying attention to the language as well as to its meaning, involves us in unnecessary distractions; and that, moreover, the stopping and starting we tend to do breaks our concentration, permitting our minds to wander. We need to ignore the fact that language divides a passage up into complex, interrelated clauses and develop our concentration so that it is fully and continuously focused on the key units of underlying meaning. The rhythm of speed reading aids our concentration and so our comprehension.

Reading slowly and carefully is not a prescription for comprehension, it is only a prescription for day-dreaming.

Sean Adam, World Speed Reading Champion

Most of us are able to increase our average reading speed from 200 to 600 words per minute with little effort. Firstly, we need to make sure that the act of reading is continuous. Try not to break off from any passages as you read them. Use a pointer, such as a pencil, to train your eyes to keep a steady track along the words on each line and move swiftly from one line to the next. A good way to test whether or not you are moving your eyes correctly is to point your finger out in front and use it to guide your eyes smoothly across the room. Now have a go at scanning the room without pointing – you will notice the more staccato movement immediately.

When you speed-read, rest the pointer on the page just below the first line of text and move it from left to right so that your eyes are able to follow the pointer along the text without pausing. Keep to a smooth and steady pace. Gradually increase the speed with which you move the pointer.

Checking the Sense

EXERCISE NINETEEN

When we speed-read we can ensure that we are focusing fully on the words by testing our comprehension of the text.

1. Determine your existing reading speed. Time yourself as you read normally through the "Left Brain, Right Brain" text on pp.30–31. Divide the number of words on the page (595) by the time it took you to read them (round up or down to the nearest minute).

2. Answer the following to check your comprehension: what name is given to the network of fibres between the two halves of the brain? which side of the brain is involved in parallel processing? where is our memory of how to play an instrument stored?

3. Now use the speed reading method to read the main text of Theories of Forgetting (pp.52–3). It contains 427 words. Time yourself and calculate your new average.

4. Test your comprehension. What is proactive inhibition? Why does retroactive inhibition seem to be more persistent? What is "trace decay"? As a rough guide your understanding should at least be the same, if not better, than with the normally read passage. Keep practising, asking a friend to set you questions on the other passages.

Quick-fix Retrieval

The tip-of-the-tongue phenomenon is a common experience. We are certain we know something – a name, a place, a quotation, a fact – and yet we cannot quite apprehend the answer. When the answer does surface, it seems to arrive suddenly out of nowhere, often minutes or hours after our attempt to remember it. If only there were methods to trigger this effect – to sort of finesse the memory into surfacing – we might avoid considerable frustration.

There are various possible ways to coax a memory out of stubborn forgetfulness, though none of them is guaranteed. Part of the secret is to avoid trying too hard, as this tends to be self-defeating, as if the memories were shy creatures, scared off by large and elaborate traps. Instead of forcing the memory, you might use guile to persuade it to approach. The way to encourage a timid cat to come to you is to ignore it. Think of your memories in the same way and distract yourself – go and do something else for a while, even something as simple as making a hot drink or reading a newspaper.

You might also try templates for size. A memory template is an "educated guess" that you measure against the lost memory to see if you sense a correspondence. Obviously, if you are searching for, say, a name, the odds against your selecting it by chance are high, but if you try your template for fit, you may feel that it is in some way partially right. If so, do you have a hunch that it has the right number of syllables? Does it begin with the right letter? Has it the right "ambience" about it? If you do sense a partial correspondence, allow it to sit in your mind without forcing it. Just wait to see if the association is strong enough to pull the memory into consciousness.

Clearing the Sea-bed of Memory

EXERCISE TWENTY

There are various ways to coax a stubborn memory out of hiding, but this exercise focuses on the idea that if we can clear our mind of clutter, our seemingly elusive quarry may surface, as if of its own accord.

1. Find a calm and quiet place in which to do this exercise – perhaps in your garden or your bedroom. Make yourself comfortable, breathe slowly and relax.

2. Try to regard the object of your search as a destination, rather than a problem – remember that concentrating too hard on trying to bring a memory to mind is as good as pushing it away altogether. Trust that the answer will come to you.

3. Close your eyes and imagine your thoughts rising from the deep and drifting away on the tide, one by one. In your mind's eye, watch them disappear over your mental horizon – they need not concern you now, because you can catch up with them later.

4. Now that your mind is clear, the memory has the opportunity to surface. Don't try to bring it to consciousness, simply remain where you are, relaxing in the peace of your surroundings. With any luck, the next item to surface will be the answer you seek.

CHAPTER SIX

THE MEMORY PALACE

Gain fulfilment through memory

Improving our memory can enrich many aspects of our lives. Even the small conveniences and satisfactions of a good memory – the ability to recall a phone number with ease, or to give pleasure by remembering a birthday – can build our confidence in ourselves. If we coach our memory to be more efficient, we also hone our concentration, focusing more on what really matters – from the information we glean from family and friends to the current affairs of our home town and beyond. We gain the potential to be more effective at work or in our studies, more organized and happier in our private lives. We can even find ways to recover lost details from our past – a store of memories that helps us understand the journey we have travelled to reach the place where we now stand – our own complex self, rich in experience, yet living fully in the now. All these aspects are covered in this chapter, which concludes with a postscript on the future of memory training in relation to new research with which I am privileged to be involved.

Living Through Detail

The more ambitious approaches to memorization, such as the journey method, train not only the memory but also the power of concentration. If I am sitting in a public hall with 20 other competitors trying to memorize the order of 20 randomly shuffled decks of cards – 1,040 pieces of data – I do not have a second to wonder if I will have time to mail a letter. Concentration must be total, or part of the mind's capacity is wasted.

Concentration training, followed through into daily life, sharpens our awareness of the world around us, and enriches our experience. Imagine that you are going for a hike in the country, alone. You might be so preoccupied with your personal concerns that you spend the whole walk wrapped in your own inner world. Or you might alternate between your own thoughts and the sense impressions that crowd in from all sides. Or you might be wholly alert to what the senses tell you, grounded in the present – and hence able to catch a glimpse of the woodpecker whose drumming you faintly hear, or to notice a nestling orchid. It would take a dedicated naturalist to hike without a single thought about home or work. Yet the point I wish to make is that concentration on the outer world brings its rewards – opportunities to relish the pleasures of the senses, and also to put personal issues into a wider perspective.

Living in the details also benefits our relationships. With our partner, our family and our friends we are engaged in a constant multiple traffic of data, and we are the poorer for every precious remark lost. With acquaintances, just remembering a name gives pleasure. Think how much generosity you can

bestow by referring back in a conversation to what this person told you about themselves three months ago. Absorbing details of your partner's changing circumstances strengthens a bond, just as failing to listen or to notice is all too often the subject of a first quarrel.

Even household chores can become less burdensome if tackled in a spirit of total concentration. Memory training makes us more appreciative of the worth of each moment. Buddhist philosophy recommends "mindfulness" – a type of meditation in which the mind becomes centred on a single object or task. Through mindfulness we appreciate the object or task for itself – we see the beauty in a grain of rice, or the value of a mundane action such as sweeping the yard. When our minds are focused in this way, we automatically relax – mindfulness frees us from the confusion of whirling thoughts.

Memory Massage

All through our lives we are urged to live in the present or to plan for the future. But to shut ourselves off from the past is to seal off one of the chambers in the heart of our being. Our lives are incomplete if we do not recognize the value of memory as an important and positive dimension of ourselves. It can help us understand who we are, what we have become, and why.

Improved memory is one of the routes to greater satisfaction in life – certainly socially and professionally, but also in terms of cultural and spiritual fulfilment, which become more profound as we accumulate experience. When problems in the present or worries about the future cause us to feel under pressure, positive reminiscences can help to improve our mood and put our concerns into perspective. Although the past is no place to live, there is no reason why we cannot draw upon it to lift our spirits.

Calling upon our senses to entice happy memories to the light of consciousness is a wonderful way to connect with the restorative episodes of our past. Try relaxing in a sensual "memory massage" session with a partner or friend, as described below. It can be refreshing either to receive or to give a massage in an ambience that encourages us to recapture lost times, or revitalize fading mental pictures. During the massage, we can allow ourselves to "soak" in our pleasant recollections as well as enjoy our partner's memories.

Set the scene by choosing a warm, comfortable and softly lit room, where you will not be disturbed. The most soothing form of memory massage is effleurage – firm but gentle stroking movements – which is suitable not only for large areas such as the back but also more delicate regions, including the face. As your partner gently massages your body, invite your most pleasant memories into your consciousness. Talking gently with the rhythm of your partner's strokes, speak openly of the memories that drift into your head. Let the fluid strokes of the massage be a cue for your memories to unloosen and flow – let them wash back to the shore of the present, like beautifully shaped driftwood on an incoming tide.

Memory in a Bottle

Smell is an extremely potent memory trigger. Not only can the use of scented candles or aromatherapy oils enhance the relaxing atmosphere of a massage, they may also evoke vivid memories. Smooth a few drops of an essential oil (diluted in two teaspoons of a base oil, such as almond oil) into the skin in slow, rhythmic strokes, or you could burn some in an oil burner. Rosemary oil is renowned for its anti-amnesiac properties (but avoid it if you are pregnant). Basil and lemon are also thought to help memory recall. (I always take a bottle of lemon essential oil with me to competitions: its aroma helps my memory and soothes my state of mind.) Sandalwood will encourage contemplation and open up creative thought. According to Hindu yogis, it has aphrodisiac properties, and therefore might be suitable for inducing erotic memories.

Dealing with Life's Demands

Some people might say that having a brilliant memory has its disadvantages. If we can remember everything that we have to do, will this increase feelings of stress? In a world of high-pressure working, with demands being made on us at all levels, we might imagine that we want to hold less in our brain, not more.

Try to banish such thoughts from your mind. The secret of coping with the external demands made upon us is to see them not as pressures but as environmental factors. They are external to us, and can never make an impact on our sense of ourselves and of our self-worth – unless we let them. By organizing ourselves, being tidy about our filing and correspondence, and prioritzing judiciously, we equip ourselves in the optimum way to do whatever is required of us. If your memory becomes hyperefficient, so much the better. An expanded memory in no sense means an expanded capacity for anxiety or confusion. It is not what we grasp in our lives that causes stress, it is what we fail to grasp.

One aspect of tuning the mind generally, in parallel with memory training, is the avoidance of worry. It takes only a few moments' thought to see how counterproductive worrying is. If something is weighing heavily upon you, take a few minutes out for a memory meditation. Pick a positive memory (perhaps a romantic dinner with your partner or a tranquil sunset). Distil this into a single symbol, then focus inwardly on the symbol, visualizing it in detail. Imagine that all the positive emotions of that time are emitted from it, like rays of light, bathing you in their sustaining glow. Open your eyes and refocus, refreshed, on your day's tasks.

The Interview Journey

EXERCISE TWENTY-ONE

One of the most stressful environments in which we find ourselves is an interview. When we feel judged, the pressure of needing to do well can weigh heavily upon us. We forget key points that will help our case, and we might also forget what we are told about the job. The following tips will focus your mind for an interview and help you succeed.

1. Breathing or meditation exercises before the interview can help to put you into a more relaxed state of mind.

2. Use memory techniques to fix in your mind 10 key points about yourself – positive qualities that equip you for the job under discussion, as well as key questions you want to ask. You might find the peg system is more appropriate than the journey method, because you will have no control of the interview's agenda.

3. When you ask questions, concentrate fully on the answers. Try to visualize each key piece of information you are given – perhaps linking it with a memorable surreal image. After the interview, note down what you remember. You may be called for a second interview, where this information could be useful.

Time Travelling

After practising memory techniques over a long period, we become adept at storing and retrieving new information. But what about all those memories that have gone before? The past is an important part of our character: it defines who we are.

I like very much people telling me about their childhood. But they'll have to be quick or I'll tell them about mine.

Dylan Thomas
1914–53

Time travelling, or pulling back the curtain of lost time, is one of my favourite memory exercises. Its purpose is to return us to a particular time and location in our past, so that we remember the experience as richly as possible. We start with a single detail and work from there, gradually building up a picture by exploratory, step-by-step association. If we open up our minds, in a suitably quiet, comfortable, dimly lit room, we may be able in time to conjure even sounds, textures, tastes, scents and emotions. For example, try to remember individual sounds – a squeaky chair, a door creaking, a crackling fire. Work from a detail that is clear to you – let's say a loudly ticking longcase clock in your grandparents' entrance hall. Think of the sound of the longcase clock as it chimed. Any visitor to the house would have passed by this clock. What would it have felt like walking up the path to the front door, entering the hall, and looking up at it as a child? What emotions did the clock evoke? As you imagine it, are the hands set to any particular time? What did your grandparents routinely do at that hour?

You might attempt a Mind Map of your childhood (see pp.112–13), starting with the homes you lived in and your relatives' homes. Probe others' memories too – just one recollection from another witness can spark a whole chain of new associations in your own mind.

Harnessing Schooldays

EXERCISE TWENTY-TWO

This exercise will set you off on your own personal trip back to your most formative years. Use class photos, old schoolbooks, trophies, and so on, to help prompt your memories.

1. Choose a location that conjures up a variety of incidental recollections, such as your old school itself. Find a specific starting point, such as a flagpole in the playground, the basketball court or the principal's office.

2. Now climb inside this mental picture. How old are you? Who are your friends? What are you wearing? What funny or scary incidents do you remember?

3. Radiate outward from your chosen point. Can you picture your classroom and where you sat? Recall individual sounds, such as the school band practising, the cheering on the football field, the squeak of the chalk on the blackboard. Can you hear a teacher's voice? What about smells – your locker or the cafeteria? Go through each of the senses in turn.

4. Now think about how you felt. Which classes did you like or dislike? Were your teachers strict or kind? Did you feel happy, anxious, bored? Carry your composite image of your school around in your head for a while, to see what other memories surface.

Releasing the Past

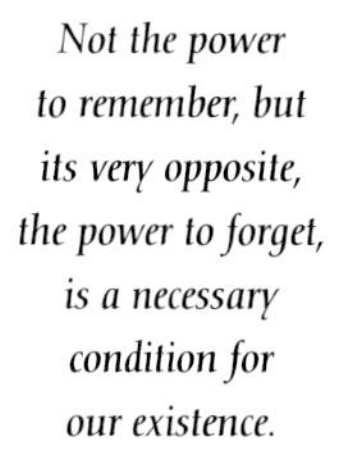

While positive recollections enrich our lives, negative ones can nag at our peace of mind in a way that is wasteful, and even destructive. Even though we know that we cannot change the past by dwelling on it, we may feel fettered somehow to our bad experiences, or our mistakes or regrets. How can we rid ourselves of such burdens?

Intense emotional experience has the effect of fixing a memory – like a fixative that prevents paint from being smudged. If we can learn to divest a memory of its emotional charge, so that the emotion does not come flooding back with recollection, then the incident that plagues us is less likely to keep surfacing in our mind.

Not the power to remember, but its very opposite, the power to forget, is a necessary condition for our existence.

Sholem Asch
1939

We need to look at upsetting memories in a practical light. Letting go of a negative experience does not mean we have to wipe clean part of our consciousness in a deliberate act of repression, merely that we need a change of perspective. It helps to think of the past as an academy of practical wisdom, based on all our experience, positive and negative. A error of judgment, no less than a personal achievement, belongs in the archive of this academy, as a compass by which you have set future directions in life. It is not a matter of debit and credit – instead, picture all the archive files bound in covers of the same colour, chronologically.

Bear in mind also that the past is a distant landscape, an unalterable vista, and we should no more wish to change parts of it than we should wish Himalayan peaks to be covered with trees. We do not live in the past: its incidents excite no emotion.

Disarming a Memory

EXERCISE TWENTY-THREE

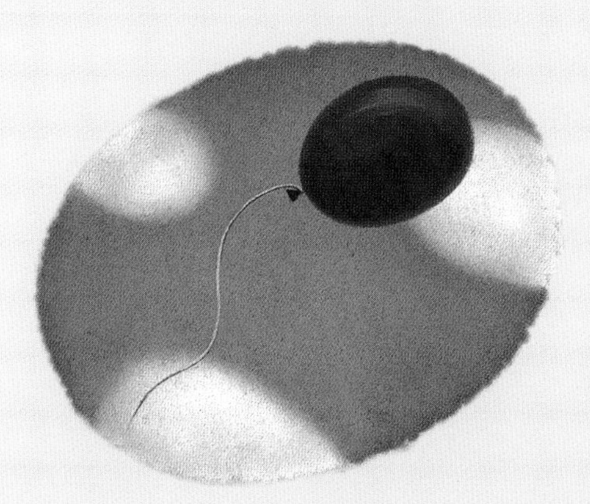

After something distressing has happened, try to deal with the negative memory before it has a chance to get lodged in the mind as an emotional transmitter. This exercise offers an effective first-aid device. You can do it at any time after the incident – whether five minutes or several hours afterward, the next day, or later.

1. Call up the memory of exactly what happened. Mentally try to put it into words as well as pictures. Identify any emotions this recollection provokes. Formulate the precise reason for these emotions.

2. Take a deep breath and make a long, slow exhalation. As you exhale imagine that you are blowing up a balloon. The out-breath carries all the negative emotions attached to the memory and, as you blow out, they fill the balloon. Imagine tying a knot in the balloon and setting it free. The memory is now free from bad feelings.

3. Imagine viewing the memory in a clear light. Think about it in only practical, logical terms. What went wrong? How it was put right (or how might you put it right)? If the experience were a messenger, what message would it carry? Finally, imagine filing away the memory in an archive. There will be no need to refer to this file again.

The World of Emotions

What are your most vivid memories? In answer to this question, most people will probably refer to personal episodes that carry a charged emotional significance. Emotional associations drive such incidents more firmly into our minds, often making them indelible. We recall the experience in high relief – albeit through the distorting lens of subjectivity.

There is a scientific reason for this advanced level of retention. Scientists believe that emotional memories are processed in a region next to the hippocampus (see p.42) in the centre of the brain, called the *amygdala*. This is a tiny almond-shaped structure, which is known to regulate our emotions. During emotional experiences (good or bad) the amygdala releases stress-related hormones, which cause the heart to pump faster, thus increasing the amount of oxygen sent to the brain, which makes memorization more efficient. Later, at the stage of recall, the amygdala stimulates a physical emotional reaction, which consequently triggers a memory. We hear a tune, feel overcome with longing, and then recall that the tune is one that was once played to us by a long-lost lover. Memory follows in the wake of reactivated emotion.

An experience may be so exciting emotionally as almost to leave a scar on the cerebral tissue.

William James
1890

Positive emotions can also be evoked by sensory triggers. Looking alone at a sunset, we may feel unaccountably contented, which might be an aesthetic satisfaction, or it might be associated with previous sunsets, perhaps when tender words were spoken. Such feelings tend to be less readily recaptured, but the exercise opposite offers one suggested approach.

Rekindling the Flame

EXERCISE TWENTY-FOUR

There is no official list of positive emotions, but a fairly loose list might include happiness, love, empathy, wonder, laughter, trust, optimism. When life seems a little flat, we can benefit by recapturing some of the emotions of the past in order to resensitize our responses.

1. Let us say that you are feeling unsympathetic to a friend, for no apparent reason. Recall as vividly as you can the last time you felt close intimacy with that friend – perhaps it was a time when the person was having a tough time, or when he or she was showing admirable qualities.

2. Visualize a gold trophy, the kind that sports players receive. This one has been specially made to commemorate your friend's special qualities, as shown on that occasion.

3. Imagine yourself in the present, taking your friend by surprise by presenting the trophy to them. You feel proud of the acquaintance you have with them. All your dissatisfactions fall away. In your mind make a little ceremonial speech of thanks, explaining why the friend deserves the trophy.

Keeping the Mind Young

People age in different ways and at different rates. Those who aspire to slow down aging might decide to eat various healthy foods, or to swim everyday at the age of 65. But if we want to keep ourselves young, we must pay attention to the mind as well as the body.

To be able to enjoy one's past is to live twice.

Martial
86CE

One important dimension to keeping the mind and memory stretched to their full potential is interest – the degree to which we are engaged with all that goes on around us, from the local scale up to the global. Interest, as much as concentration, provides a firm grounding for effective memorization. When we are children, so much is exciting because we have never seen it before. As we get older we are in danger of becoming jaded – we tend to be less fascinated by our surroundings. The secret of regaining our excitement is to look through the veil of the familiar to what lies beyond, to be alert to the surprises all around us, to see the intriguing connections that give a shape to our experiences and encounters. We must never take the world for granted: look at the moon through binoculars and identify the craters; learn the species of trees in your local park; visit an exhibition of flower paintings to learn about the Dutch tulip trade of the seventeenth century, when tulips were used as currency.

Aging must not be thought of as the inevitable harbinger of memory loss (see p.58). Once we reject expectations that our minds will begin to fail us as we get older, we can look positively to the future. Our memories become richer as we continue to gain new experiences in a spirit of active inquiry and engagement.

Tracing Connections

EXERCISE TWENTY-FIVE

Knowledge does not exist in isolation. By tracing connections from one subject to another and filling in the context, you begin to gain a more complete understanding. The information becomes more meaningful, more interesting, and hence more memorable.

1. Place leisure activities in context by learning about their background – not only through books but also through observation. A gardener might read up on the plant finders who in time past discovered and collected plants he or she is now growing, as well as keeping a diary of his or her own garden, with notes on flowering times, wildlife, and so on.

2. Place world news in the perspective of its historical background. There is no clean separation between history and current affairs. History is happening now, all over the world, as we read this book. Trace present events to their origins in the past.

3. When you come across a coincidence – two different sources mentioning the same name or information – take this as a sign that it might be worth delving further into the subject. In a biography, for example, you are sure to read about the subject's family and friends – do some biographical research into these figures.

Memory of the Future

Competitors who take part in the annual Mind Sports Olympiad (of which the World Memory Championship is one part), whether they are competing at chess, memory, bridge or speed reading, are now being referred to as "mentathletes". This term reflects a growing public fascination with the true potential of our brains.

At the same time, it is being increasingly realized that feats of memory are not merely conjuring tricks, or attempts born out of sheer perseverance and application to make a name in the record books – like someone who has spent an unprecedented length of time in a phone box. No, memory champions demonstrate something much more significant than this: the perfectibility of mental capacity, the scientifically important fact that the brain can do far more work than most people realize. Nature's gift of the mind is richer and more brilliant than anything most of us have ever dreamed of.

It is reassuring that, in an age where technological innovation is massively dominated by computers, to make communal and personal information available through smarter and smarter software, there is a corner of our thoughts still devoted to the time-honoured topic of human memory. Even as you read, exciting new discoveries are being made in a handful of research labs across the globe. It is to be hoped that cognitive and psychological studies will continue to be pursued with

everyday practical applications in mind – in particular, the question of which techniques work best for storing and retrieving specific types of information.

What we can be fairly sure about is that none of us needs "gimmicks" (such as portable computers and pocket organizers) to be able to remember – just a will and a way. All we memory champions can do, for the moment at least, is pass on the techniques that we have learned by a long process of experiment and refinement. I like to think that we are pioneers, not conjurers. What conjurer would so willingly reveal the backstage workings of his tricks to a curious audience? In time, I hope that there will be more and more of us who can open up new rooms in the memory palace and pocket the treasures within.

Brainwave 1 Machine

The Brainwave 1 machine was developed by the Alpha-learning Institute based in Switzerland. The greatest minds in history, from Leonardo da Vinci to Albert Einstein, were those who used both sides of their brain effectively. This latest technology helps us to achieve a mental balance in our everyday thoughts. It involves wearing a pair of glasses with light-emitting diodes – LEDs – that pulsate at varying speeds. At the same time headphones are worn that emit a beat synchronized to the pulsing lights. The combination of light and sound trains the brain to "tune in" to the optimum frequencies for concentration and relaxation, and balance the brain waves of both hemispheres. Currently, only a few people are aware of this technology. My hope is that in the future it will be used to benefit everyone in all types of industry – from business to sports – and especially in education.

Bibliography

Abrahams, Roger D. ed.
African American Folktales: Stories from Black Traditions in the New World
Pantheon Books (New York), 1985

Ashcraft, Mark H.
Human Memory and Cognition, Second Edition
HarperCollins (London) and Addison-Wesley (Reading, Massachussetts), 1994

Baddeley, Alan
Your Memory, A User's Guide
Prion (London) and Allyn & Bacon (Needham Heights, Massachussetts), 1998

Bloom, Floyd E. and Lazerson, Arlyne
Brain, Mind, and Behavior
W.H. Freeman and Co. (Basingstoke, UK and New York), 1988

Buzan, Tony and Buzan, Barry
The Mind Map Book
BBC Books (London) and Plume Books (New York), 1996

Buzan, Tony
Use Your Memory
BBC Books (London) and Penguin Books (New York), 1992

Cade, C. Maxwell and Coxhead, Nona
The Awakened Mind
Element (Shaftesbury, Dorset and Rockport, Massachussetts), 1989

Crook, Thomas H. and Adderly, Brenda
The Memory Cure
Thorsons (London and San Francisco), 1999

Crossley-Holland, Kevin ed.
Northern Lights: Legends, Sagas and Folk-tales
Faber and Faber Ltd (London), 1987

Dudley, Geoffrey A.
Double Your Learning Power
Thorsons (London and San Francisco), 1986

Fidlow, Michael
Strengthen Your Memory
Foulsham & Co Ltd (Cippenham, UK), 1991

Fry, Ron
Improve Your Memory
Kogan Page (London), 1997

Gatti, Anne
Tales from the African Plains
Pavilion Books Ltd (London) and Puffin (New York), 1997

Greenfield, Susan
The Human Brain, A Guided Tour
Phoenix (Oxford, UK) and Basic Books (New York), 1997

Gruneberg, Michael M. and Herrmann, Douglas J.
Your Memory for Life
Blandford (London) and Sterling Publishing (New York), 1997

Houston, Jean
The Possible Human
J.B. Tarcher (New York), 1982

Hull, Robert
Central and South American Stories
Tales from Around the World series
Wayland Ltd (Hove, UK), 1994

Lawson, John and Silver, Harold
A Social History of Education in England
Methuen (London), 1973

O'Brien, Dominic
How to Develop a Perfect Memory
Pavilion (London), 1993

O'Brien, Dominic
How to Pass Exams
Headline (London), 1995

O'Brien, Dominic
Super Memory Power (Books 1–4)
Linguaphone (London), 1997

Ostrander, Sheila and Schroeder, Lynn
Cosmic Memory: The Supermemory Revolution
Souvenir Press (London), 1991

Parkin, Alan J.
Memory – Phenomena, Experiment and Theory
Psychology Press (Hove, UK), 1993

Rose, Steven
The Making of Memory
Bantam Books (London and New York), 1993

Russell, Peter
The Brain Book
Routledge (London) and Penguin (New York), 1997

Samuel, David
Memory – How We Use It, Lose It and Can Improve It
Weidenfeld & Nicolson (London) and New York University Press (New York), 1999

Schacter, Daniel L.
Searching for Memory
Basic Books (London) and HarperCollins (New York), 1996

Wingfield, Arthur and Byrnes, Dennis L.
The Psychology of Human Memory
Academic Press (London and Chestnut Hill, Massachussetts), 1981

Yates, Frances A.
The Art of Memory
Pimlico (London) and University of Chicago Press (Chicago), 1994

Index

A

acronyms 94–5
active memory *see* short-term memory
Ad Herennium 18
aging
  exercise of memory 59, 150–51
  memory loss and 58–9, 150
alcohol intake, and memory loss 55
Allport, G.W. 57
Alphalearning Institute 153
amnesia *see* memory loss
anchoring, location technique 65–6, 75
animals, and memory 37
anxiety *see* worry
Aristotle 17, 68
aromatherapy, and memory recall 141
association 46, 65–7, 72–3, 88, 90, 126, 128
  Aristotle and 15
  DOMINIC system and 108–9
  facial recognition and 116–17
  journey method 102–7
  mnemonics 94
  number-shape system 110–11, 129
  recalling the past 144
  visual pegs 96, 102

B

babies and memory 56
brain, the
  beneficial foods 83
  emotional memories 154
  functioning 40–43
  left and right brains 30–31, 64–5, 68, 88–9, 153
  memory retention 21, 22, 26–8, 31, 32, 40–43, 64–5
  memory training and 62–3
  rhythms 32–3
  structure 26–8, 30, 148
  see also rhythm
brain waves 32–3, 77, 153
Brainwave 1 machine 153
breathing
  memorization 33
  negative memories 147
  stress 143
Brown, Roger 45
Bruno, Giordano 20
Buddhism, mindfulness and 139
Buzan, Tony 112

C

Camillo, Giulio 19, 20
card games, memory and 125–7
cardcounting 125
chess, memory and 124–5
children, and memory 56–7
chunking, learning strategy 51
Cicero, Marcus Tullius 18
comprehension, reading and 131, 133
computers 23, 40
concentration
  benefits of 138–9
  memorization 46, 76–7, 88
consciousness, memory and 23
context-dependent memory 90–91
creative thought 65, 70
  brain and 26–7
crossword puzzles 121

D

dates, remembering 118–19
De Oratore (Cicero) 18
death, and memory loss 14
declarative memory 36–8
  in children 56–7
déjà vu 53
Dennett, Daniel 23
diary, mental 119
diet, and memory 83
DOMINIC system 80, 108–9, 124, 126
dreams 48–9

E

Ebbinghaus, Hermann 50

education *see* learning
eidetic memory 57
emotions
  brain and 26, 148
  memory retention 148
  negative memories 146
  recall of 144, 148, 149
encephalitis, and memory loss 55
engrams 42
environment, memory and 90–91
episodic memories 37
etymology, as aid to memory 120
events, memory of 37
exercise
  memory training and 49, 62–3, 67, 150–51
  physical fitness and 82
explicit memory *see* declarative memory

F

faces, recognition of 29, 116–17
factual memory 37
fitness and health, memory and 82–3
flashbulb memories 45
foods, for brain and memory 82–3
forgetting *see* memory loss
Freud, Sigmund 10

G

games *see* card games; chess
genetic memories 37
Ginkgo biloba leaves 49, 82
Goethe, Johann Wolfgang von 82
Greeks, mnemonic techniques 16–17, 18, 23, 65, 74, 94

H

health and fitness, memory and 82–3
hearing
  sensory memory 34–5
  see also sound
Homer 14–15
hypnosis, and memory recall 55

I

icons, in the visual cortex 35
Iliad (Homer) 15
imagination
  Aristotle's views on 68
  journey method 102
  memory and 65–7, 68–71, 126, 128
  visual pegs 96
implicit memory *see* procedural memory
information retrieval 88–91, 152–3
  stress and 46
intelligence, and memory 51
interest, maintenance of in age 150–51
interviews 96, 143
IQ, and memory 51

J

Jaensch, E.R. 57
"jizz", recognition and 29
journey method 102–7
  card games 125–7
  chess 124–5
  concentration training 138–9
  educational learning 21, 23, 128–9
  location technique 75, 102
  number memorization 111
  remembering dates 118–19
  speeches and 106–7, 122–3
  see also location

K

Kihlstrom, John 10
Kulick, James 45

L

language acquisition 56–7
learning
  effective memory techniques 50–51, 128–9
  formal education 21, 23, 128–9
  rote 21, 80

lemon essential oil 141
location 16–17, 18, 65–7, 74–5, 12
concentration 76
journey method 102
visual pegs 66, 96
see also journey method
locus principle *see* location
Loftus, Elizabeth 45–6
logical thought 65
long-term memory (LTM) 35, 36–9, 42, 52
anterograde amnesia 55
old age 58–9
Lozandi, Georgi 86
Luria, Alexander 22

M

massage, and memory recall 140–41
Matteo Ricci 19
meditation
concentration and 76–7, 139
dealing with stress 142, 143
memorization and 33
pre-sleep 49
memory 64–5
benefits 136
computers and 23, 40
distortion of 44–6
encoding 39–42
external aids to 46
fount of inspiration 16
historical overview of 12–23
improvement of 60–91
memory chains 99
memory forest keyboard 97
memory theatres 19, 20
memory tree (*Ginkgo biloba*) 49, 82
memory wheels 20
negative memories 146–7
recall triggers 34, 95, 134–5, 141, 144, 145
reliability of 44–7
templates 134
three keys of 65, 126
training of 59, 62–3, 67, 152–3
twentieth-century studies of 22–3, 36, 59, 152–3
types 18, 34–9
Memory Forum 47
memory loss
aging and 58–9, 150
amnesia 54–5
death and 16
forgetting 52–3
short-term memory and 36, 55
mental imaging 65, 66, 68–71, 109
negative memories and 147
see also visualization
Miller, George, memory chunks 51
mind
clearing clutter from 135
conscious and unconscious 31, 36, 38, 56
Mind Maps 112–13, 122–3
of childhood 144
reading and 130, 131
Mind Sports Olympiad 112, 152
mnemonics
ancient techniques 16–18, 23
linguistic 128
word-based 66, 94–5
Mnemosyne, goddess of memory 16, 94
"morphing" 71
Muses 16
music
aid to memorization 86–7
brain activity and 31
see also sound
myths and legends 15

N

names, memory of 29, 36–7, 96, 116–17
neurotransmitters 28, 42
see also brain,
numbers
digit span test 43
DOMINIC system 80, 108–9, 124, 126
mnemonics 95
number-shape system 80, 110–11, 129

O

observation, as memory aid 78–9
oral traditions 14–15
oratory 18
see also speeches
Oxford World Reading Programme 120

P

past, the
  dealing with negative
    memories of 146–7
  recall of 140–41, 144–5
peg system 66, 96–7, 128
  combatting stress 143
permanent memory *see*
    long-term memory
photographic memory 57
PIN-numbers, memorization
    110–11
planets, memorization exercise
    101
Plato, ideas about memory 20,
    24
proactive inhibition 52–3
procedural memory 36, 38–9,
    55

Q

Quintilian 18

R

reading 130–31
  speed reading 132–3
recall 88–91
  effect of stress 45–6
  number 110–11
  past and 144–5
  surprise random 91
  triggering 95, 134–5, 141, 144,
    145
  word 120–21
recognition, names and faces
    29, 116–17
reference memory *see*
    long-term memory
religion, memory training
    19–20
REM sleep 48–9
repetition, retention and 67,
    80–81
retroactive inhibition 52–3
revision
  retention and 67, 80–81, 88
  rule of five 81, 123
rhetoric 18
  see also speeches
rhyme, mnemonics and 95
rhythm, mnemonics and
    95
Ricci, Matteo 19
Rigveda 15
Romans, mnemonic techniques
    18, 23, 74

S

scents
  memory and 84
  recall of 141, 144
semantic memory 37–8
  in children 56–7
senses, memorization and 17,
    22, 34–6, 69, 78–9, 84–5, 91,
    123
sensory memories 34–6
Shereshevsky, Luria's tests 22
shopping lists 106–7
short-term memory (STM) 35,
    36, 40–41, 43, 51
  anterograde amnesia and
    55
  in children 56
  in old age 58
sight, and memory 34–5,
    78–9, 84, 91
Simonides of Ceos 16
skills, procedural memory and
    38–9, 50
sleep
  brain rhythms 32
  memory and 48–9
smell, and recall 34, 84, 91, 123,
    141
sound
  recall and 34, 84, 85, 91, 123
  see also hearing; music
sounds, recall of 144
speeches 96, 106–7, 122–3
  see also oratory, rhetoric
"Speed Cards" 125–7
speed reading 152–3
story method 98–101
storytelling 15
stress
  coping with 142–3
  expanded memory and 142
  recall and 45–6
stroke, and memory loss 55
surprise random recall 91
synesthesia 22

T

taste, and memory 34, 84
tastes, recall of 144
textures, recall of 144
time travelling 144–5
total-time hypothesis 50
touch, and memory 34, 85
trace-decay theory 52

V

Vedic tradition 15
violence, memories of 45–6
visual pegs *see* peg system
visualization 69–71, 85, 111, 123, 128–9, 143
  dealing with stress 142–3
  journey method and 102–7
  past and 144–5
  recall of positive emotions 149
  story method and 98–101
  see also mental imaging
vitamin B_1 deficiency 55

W

walking, journey method 105
words, recall of 120–21
working memory *see* short-term memory
World Memory Championships 49, 66, 74, 92, 152
worry, memory and 59, 142

Acknowledgments

The author and publishers would like to thank Tony Buzan for his permission to use the Mind Map®™ technique in this book.

For further information about Mind Maps®™, please contact the Buzan Centre at the following places:

UK
54 Parkstone Road
Poole
Dorset
BH15 2PG
Telephone: 01202 674676
Fax: 01202 674776

US
P.O. Box 4
Palm Beach
Florida 33480
Telephone: (561) 881 0188

On the Web
www.Mind-Map.com

Email
buzan@Mind-Map.com

The author would also like to thank Sean Adam of the Alphalearning Institute for his inspirational work.